ALSO BY JEFF SMITH

The Frugal Gourmet (1984)

The Frugal Gourmet Cooks with Wine (1986)

The Frugal Gourmet Cooks American (1987)

The Frugal Gourmet Cooks Three Ancient Cuisines (1989)

The Frugal Gourmet on Our Immigrant Ancestors (1990)

BY JEFF SMITH AND CRAIG WOLLAM

The Culinary Handbook (1991)

The Frugal Gourmet
Celebrates Christmas

T H E

Frugal Gourmet

CELEBRATES

Christmas

Jeff Smith

Craig Wollam
Culinary Consultant

Terrin Haley
D. C. Smith
Research Assistants

Photography by Louis Wallach
Woodcuts by David Frampton

William Morrow and Company, Inc.
New York

Grateful acknowledgment is made to the following for use of material in this book:

"Journey of the Magi" from *Collected Poems, 1909–1962* by T. S. Eliot. Copyright 1936 by Harcourt Brace Jovanovich, Inc., copyright © 1964, 1963 by T. S. Eliot. Reprinted by permission of the publisher.

Recipes for Yorkshire Pudding and Candied Orange and Lemon Peel reprinted by permission of Macmillan Publishing Company from *The Joy of Cooking* by Irma S. Rombauer and Marion Rombauer Becker. Copyright © 1931, 1936, 1941, 1942, 1943, 1946, 1951, 1952, 1953, 1962, 1963, 1964, 1975 by The Bobbs-Merrill Co., Inc.

Recipe for Tzimmes reprinted courtesy of *Sunset* magazine.

Santa Claus by Norman Rockwell. Copyright © 1939 by the Norman Rockwell Family Trust. Reprinted by permission of the Norman Rockwell Family trust.

Illustrations of Santa Claus (1931 and 1947) by Haddon Sundblom. Reprinted courtesy of the Archives, The Coca-Cola Company.

Santa Answers a Call in Shop and *Merry Old Santa Claus* by Thomas Nast. Reprinted courtesy of The Bettmann Archive.

"Christmas Oratorio" from *Collected Poems of W. H. Auden.* Copyright © 1976 by Edward Mendelson, William Meredith, and Monroe K. Spears, executors of the estate of W. H. Auden. Reprinted by permission of Random House, Inc.

Pages 258 and 259 plates provided by Ceramica, 59 Thompson Street, New York, N.Y. 10012.

Copyright © 1991 by Frugal Gourmet, Inc.

Photographs copyright © 1991 by Louis B. Wallach, Inc.

Woodcuts copyright © 1991 by David Frampton

Library of Congress Cataloging-in-Publication Data

Smith, Jeff.
    The frugal gourmet celebrates Christmas: the history of the season's traditions, with recipes for the feast / Jeff Smith ; Craig Wollam, culinary consultant ; Terrin Haley, D.C. Smith, research assistants ; food photography by Louis Wallach ; woodblock prints by David Frampton.
      p.   cm.
    Includes bibliographical references and index.
    ISBN 0-688-09128-8
    1. Christmas cookery. 2. Christmas. 3. Frugal Gourmet (Television program) I. Title.
TX739.2.C45S65   1992
641.5'68–dc20
                                        91-29768
                                        CIP

Printed in the United States of America

First Edition

1 2 3 4 5 6 7 8 9 10

BOOK DESIGN BY RICHARD ORIOLO

To
Saints Francis and Nicholaus,
who have given us
our Christmas Traditions

Acknowledgments

How do you thank and recognize those who have made your memories of Christmases past? I think of my old boy Scout troop, Troop 126, and Bert Hobbes, our scoutmaster. Every year we sold hundreds of Christmas trees, and it was a real operation. The kids in the troop who had little money traveled with us on all camping trips for the whole year, all from Christmas tree sales.

I think of the Christmas Eve service at Christ Church, in Tacoma. Each Christmas Eve I seem to be standing in the main aisle singing "O Come All Ye Faithful" and offering

thanks that I am alive for another year. One year it was heart surgery, one year it was a suspected brain tumor, one year it was . . . well, Christ Church has always been a great support to me, and I thank them. Many of the theological ideas expressed in this book were first offered from the pulpit to the loving congregation at Christ Church.

Patrick's of Bayside, a wonderful religious-supply house on Long Island, New York, found the Italian manger that glues this book together. Patrick's is a gracious firm, and I thank them.

This book came about because of the request . . . no, the prodding, of two dear friends, Bill Adler, my book agent, and Al Marchioni, president and chief executive officer of William Morrow and Company. This whole project came about during a rather mediocre Chinese dinner party in which these two suggested a Christmas book. Craig, my right hand, looked at me and with his eyes said, "No." Then I heard my voice say, "Yes." I love theology more than food. I thank Al and Bill again for their patience and support.

Maria Guarnaschelli, my editor, is to be credited with fine ideas, excellent cooking, and kind editing. She is not only a dear friend but a confidante and teacher.

Happy Holidays to those who helped us in the research of this book, particularly Terrin Haley and D. C. Smith. They came up with stories and facts that should probably make up another book. And, to the Reverend Bill Jones, a friend of many years, thanks is due for his research on and affection for the original Saint Nicholaus.

The brilliant artist who created the woodcuts for this book is David Frampton. The work is so creative, and his insights so helpful.

I have never published colored pictures of the dishes that I cook, but this time, this holiday, this Holy Time, is an exception. The pictures that make you hungry are by Louis Wallach. Thanks to him and his crew, these pictures are the best!

I want to make special mention of Richard Oriolo for the beautiful design of my book. He is a very special and talented man and I am grateful to have him work on my book.

Patty, my wife, was most helpful with her editorial comments. She is a fine theologian, and her insights always enlighten me. She offered several of our family recipes as well.

Emely Smith, my mother, offered many good things to this book, just as she offered many good things to my life. She stands with a group of family friends that made contributions as well.

Our office staff is to be thanked for each book. Dawn Sparks, my secretary, has been with me since our first cookbook was published in 1984. Need I talk to you about patience? And Jim Paddleford, our business manager, is important to our books because he knows more about what I do than I do!

Finally, I must thank Craig Wollam, my cook and right-hand support. A great friendship has developed through the years, a friendship that is strong enough that when he nods no to me about our agreeing to another cookbook, I know I can talk him into it. He is terribly patient with me, just as we all should be with one another during this wonderful but tense holiday time.

Merry Christmas to all!

Contents

Introduction

Christmas Eve is my favorite night of the year. It always has been, ever since I was a child. As far back as my memory can see, I remember the excitement, the feast, the presents—though we could open only one on the Holy Eve, all else had to wait for the Morning.

During the Second World War, when sugar was rationed and butter was impossible to find, my beloved mother, Emely, somehow produced butter cookies covered in sugar, and to this day I do not know how she came by the ingredients. Now she tells me she cannot remember.

That was one Christmas memory. And I remember how cold it was on that darkest night in Tacoma, and how my father *finally* came home from work. And then the wait. The wait until dinner was over, then the wait until he and Mom would stop talking. Oh, how the time seemed to drag on and on.

You have the same memories, I know. It is amazing how similar our childhood experiences of Christmas really are. When I was growing up, our family was not very in-volved in the Church, so I saw Christmas mainly as a won-derful party that came in the middle of the winter. I did not know what Christmas was really about at all.

After college I went off to graduate school to study theology. There I was given a new memory of Christmas. I had been studying Systematic Theology, a course in how to think in theological terms common to the Bible. John Drew Godsey taught the class. Just before Christmas break he in-vited all of us to his home, where his wife, another Emily, served us hot cider and we sang Christmas carols around the piano. Now, you cannot get any more nostalgic and old-fashioned Christmas-y than that! As we sang "O Come All Ye Faithful" and the words *"Word of the Father, now in flesh*

appearing" rang throughout the room, I was horrified. I realized it was the first time in my life that I understood the words: *"Word of the Father, Now in Flesh Appearing."* The fact that God had to go to such extremes to explain the meaning of our place together. God declares Himself/Herself to us by becoming a baby in our midst. The greatest sign of weakness, *"living flesh"* in its most vulnerable state, a tiny baby, becomes the greatest sign of the strength of the Holy One, a strength born out of love beyond our furthest imaginings, a strength that, I suppose, still looks to many of us like weakness.

That same year I met Patty, my wife. We established a family and created our own family customs . . . and Christmas was at last mine, and very different from my childhood.

This book is not about napkin folding, or Christmas table decorations, or special ways to trim Christmas trees. It is rather about Christmas, the Great Mass, or the sending us out after the feast of His birth.

For those of you who know me, you have never heard me speak so enthusiastically in Christian theological terms, but get ready. I want you, beloved reader, whether you are a typical family of four or five, or a single parent living a

life for your child, or a bachelor who loves to take care of the nieces and nephews at Christmastime, or a grandma or grandpa now living alone who still remembers the big snowstorm in December 1949—whatever your situation, I want to bring the Manger and the Donkey, the Angels, and the Blessed Mother with Child into your Christmas.

The Background

Christmas was not celebrated until quite late in the history of the Church. Oh, of course Easter was celebrated from the beginning, for it was the Resurrection that established the Church. But Christmas was not even recognized on the calendar until about the fourth century. At that time Saint John Chrysostom wrote that Pope Julius (A.D. 337–352) had commissioned Saint Cyril to undertake an investigation to determine the month and day of Christmas. December 25 was decided upon.

The celebration thus took place on this date, though we have no idea in what month or on what day the Child

was actually born. However, since it is the darkest night of the year, and since so many other Roman and pagan festivals were celebrated during the winter, such a date is perfect for our evening of "stars so brightly shining." No matter that other groups were using the same date, December 24 is the night we chose for a festival that would get us through the darkness. And we had good reason, since Christmas is all about Light coming in the midst of our darkness.

The Puritans in America were so upset about the pagan connections with the winter Christmas holiday that they had Christmas outlawed in New England. Can you believe it? But when the German and Irish immigrants moved to the new land in the mid-nineteenth century, they finally persuaded the Yankees that Christmas was acceptable.

No, our using the same times of the year as the pagan communities of northern Europe to celebrate our holidays does not bother me at all. It bothers me no more than the realization that the writers of the Old Testament, the early traditions, used many stories from the ancient world to explain their theological insights. I think that is what theology is all about. The word "theology," after all, means "God-talk," or talk about God. How you do it is not half as

important as the conclusion to which you finally come. Further, if the Queen of England can declare her birthday to be in June simply because it is a good time for tourists, then our Prince of Peace can celebrate His birthday as the Child of Light on the darkest night of the year. The date has nothing to do with the truth behind the event.

I hope you use this book to help your family better understand this profound and joyous holiday. You will find a bit of nostalgia in these pages because I cannot help it, and you will also find a recipe for everyone who appears in the traditional crèche or manger scene. There is a dish for each.

THE ADVENT

The Advent, or the "Season of the Coming," begins our celebration of Christmas. It begins on the fourth Sunday before Christmas and ends at midnight on Christmas Eve. The season is a time of preparation and contemplation on what is about to happen . . . again. Advent means, "Get ready, The Child is coming!"

What do I think about during this time? I think about the people of Ancient Israel and what they were feeling. They were awaiting the coming of their Messiah, the anointed one of God. At the time the political situation in Jerusalem

was just terrible. The Romans occupied the city and there were Roman guards and soldiers and governors everywhere. The Biblical hope of a Savior, a Messiah, had been translated into hope for a Messianic Ruler who would rid the people of these foreign invaders, these Romans. All during the life of Jesus there were battles between the Roman occupation troops and the Zealots, a group of guerrilla fighters who hid in the hills during the day and sneaked into town to fight the Romans at night. We are now fairly sure that Judas was not the bad guy in the Biblical story, but rather a Zealot, from which the word "zealous" originates. He was very eager to see the Messiah bring about a new order in Jerusalem, so eager that he told the Romans where Jesus was, thinking that Jesus, whom Judas believed to be the Messiah, would do something drastic! Instead, Jesus gave himself over to the Roman guards, and Judas, who could not believe what he had done, hanged himself. But I am getting ahead of the story.

The other thing that I think about during Advent is the ancient name of God in the Hebrew scriptures. It is beautiful beyond belief. The name, which an Orthodox Jew will not even say out loud since the name is too holy to be

uttered, is Yahweh. It means "The Holy One of Israel." The term for "Holy" is *kadosh* in Hebrew, and it means "that which is so far above man and womankind, so distant and beyond our understanding, so heavenly and unapproachable. . . ." Well, it means "beyond the beyond," never near us. The term "of Israel" means "right here in town." That is to say, "The Most Distant One is here in town with us, always." I love that! Another Biblical word for the "One That Is Coming," the Messiah, is Emmanuel, "God with Us." It means very much the same thing. The genius behind Hebrew theology is the ability to see the Godhead in our very midst, locally, and to become committed to it. Jesus, then, as being referred to as the "Son of the Most High," Emmanuel, becomes God in our midst.

That is what I think about during Advent.

You may wish to establish an Advent wreath to help your family better understand this time of preparation. Any local church can offer you a pamphlet or instruction on how to prepare one, and you can have a wonderful time with your family as the Holy Night draws nigh. Patty, Channing, Jason, and I have done that since the boys were babies. Sweet memories.

Lentils and Rice with Onions and Sesame Oil

SERVES 8

All of the ingredients in this recipe would have been common in a kitchen in Bethlehem. During your Advent preparation, you might wish to cook this in order to let your family know a bit about foods in the ancient world. It is really very good.

4 medium yellow onions, peeled
3 tablespoons olive oil
1 cup lentils
3½ cups cold water
1 cup Uncle Ben's Converted Rice
2 teaspoons salt
2 tablespoons sesame oil

Dice 3 of the onions. Heat a large frying pan and add 2 tablespoons of the olive oil and the diced onions. Sauté until quite brown; set aside.

In a 4-quart saucepan, combine the lentils and water. Bring to a boil, covered, and turn down the heat to a simmer. Cook for 10 minutes. Add the cooked onions to the lentils with the rice and the salt. Cover and simmer 20 minutes until the rice and lentils are tender. Remove from the heat and stir in the sesame oil. Slice the remaining onion into rings. Heat the frying pan again and sauté the onion rings in the remaining 1 tablespooon olive oil until tender. Serve the sautéed onion rings over the lentils and rice.

THE MANGER
AND BIRTH

Saint Francis
of Assisi

The celebration of Christmas as we know it, with presents, trees, lights, and the manger scene, is fairly recent. The good Saint Francis of Assisi in Italy is credited with the development of what we now know as the manger scene.

You remember that Saint Francis was a great lover of birds, of animals, and of all God's creation. He lived during the 1200s in Italy, in the town of Assisi after which he is

named. He seems to have been the first to come up with the idea of honoring the child with a manger scene, filled with the Saint's beloved animals.

*

For I would make a memorial of that Child who was born in Bethlehem, and in some sort behold with bodily eyes His infant hardships; how He lay in a manger on hay, with the ox and ass standing by. *

The good saint called the townspeople together and they constructed a manger scene, a scene taken from the account of Saint Luke, the only gospel writer to actually describe the birth of Jesus. You will remember the story that tells of how Joseph and his betrothed, Mary, who was with child, were called to register for a census tax that was to be paid to Rome. How insulting! So, Mary and Joseph traveled into Bethlehem because Joseph was a part of the tradition and family of that community.

---

*The words of Saint Francis, quoted in *The Life of Saint Francis of Assisi,* by Brother Thomas of Celano, 1229.

"The Nativity," Workshop of Fra Angelico,
Florentine, 1387–1455

And while they were there, the time came for her to be delivered. And she gave birth to her first-born son and wrapped him in swaddling cloths, and laid him in a manger, because there was no place for them in the inn.

A manger was really the feeding place for the cattle and other animals that the innkeeper kept for his own use. I doubt that he served food at the inn. That was not the custom. However, he was kind enough to tell these two people whom he did not even know that they could sleep with the animals. Thus begins Saint Francis's fascination with Saint Luke's account of the birth, the Nativity.

Saint Francis was such a quiet and holy man that legend has it that birds would come and rest on his shoulders. He established a wonderful order of monks who still devote themselves to a very quiet service to God and service to the poor. You can imagine what he would think about the frantic pace that we set for ourselves during Advent and Christmastide. He thought it should be a time of solemn reflection on the celebration of the birth.

My wife is fond of Saint Francis, and she recently composed a letter for our parish. She claimed the letter was written by Saint Francis himself, the founder of the Franciscan order of monks in the Church, and addressed to his dear friend Clare, a woman so influenced by Saint Francis she gave herself to monastic life and founded the order of nuns, the Poor Clares. She was declared a saint because of her kind and charitable works, as well as her spiritual devotion. Here is Patty's letter. I hope that it calms you as you prepare for Christmas.

Winter 1224

My Dear Sister Clare,

How kind of you to ask how you can help the brothers in Assisi prepare for Christmas while I am away preaching in the country.

I know there is much to be done. Food must be prepared for the many brothers and sisters who will return from their work to celebrate the feast with us. And food must be prepared to share with the poor. The townspeople will expect us to arrange another manger scene and midnight mass. We must locate animals and

torches, even a baby! We must find a priest for the mass and deacons to assist.

You know that in my heart Christmas, the feast of love, is my favorite feast—the one I wish would never end. It is the time when the poor should be treated royally, and the animals are not only welcome but necessary to our worship.

But, dear Sister Clare, do not let yourself or any one of us get caught up in the busy-ness. That is false preparation for the great Christmas feast. God would have us prepare quietly, in our hearts and in our living. We must pray and wait for the Incarnation but be prepared for it at every moment. Look at the faces of the lonely and befriend them. See Jesus in the hungry and feed them. Put seeds on the road for the birds. And stop to thank God for the beauty of the moon on a cold dark night.

This is how to prepare for Christmas.

Pax et Bonum
Your little Brother,
Francis

**Jeff's crèche, carved in the town
of Ortisei, Italy**

Thus we have the spirit of the manger scene. The most famous little figures are still carved in Italy, the carvers working throughout the spring and summer so that they are ready for the Advent season. I am told that there is a street in Naples that sells nothing but manger scenes, all animals and characters included.

The most famous manger scene that can be found in this country is on display each Advent at our wonderful Metropolitan Museum of Art in New York City. It is the eighteenth-century Neapolitan Christmas Crèche from the Loretta Hines Howard Collection. You must see it!

The pictures of the manger scene in the book are from one I own that was carved in the village of Ortisei, in the

**Full view of Christmas tree with crèche figures
in the Medieval Sculpture Hall,
Metropolitan Museum of Art, New York**

"Nativity Scene," painted wood and terracotta. Gift of
Loretta Hines Howard, 1964. Photograph by Lee Boltin

mountainous area in northern Italy not far from the Swiss border. We will go through the manger and meet each character, and I shall suggest a recipe for each. It might be fun for you and your family to make some of these dishes during your Advent preparation for the Christmas.

"The Annunciation," detail, altarpiece.
Robert Campin, Flemish, c. 1425

The Blessed
Mother Mary

In the early days of my theological education I simply could not understand the Church's devotion to Mary. Now, many years later, I realize how terribly important it is that we have and celebrate and adore the feminine aspect of the Godhead. After all, God is neither male nor female but rather androgynous, the best of both sexes. The image of God as Father traditionally stands for the strong, unwavering, justice-seeking, and rather judgmental part of God. Mary, on the other hand, stands for the more traditional feminine characteristics of God, such as the patient,

**Mary, the Baby Jesus,
and Joseph
From Jeff's crèche**

**Detail of Mary from
"The Annunciation."
Workshop of
Fra Angelico, Florentine,
1387–1455**

the nurturing, the always-there aspects of the Holy One. We need all of these traits if we are to understand the Biblical image of the Godhead.

Mary, a woman of innocence and purity, is told by an angel that she is to conceive the Son of the Most High. She responds with an innocent sort of "Who, Me?" and the child is conceived "by the Spirit, by the Word of God." Now, while it is true that she did have Joseph as her betrothed, and while it was common to sleep with a young woman prior to marriage in order to be sure that she could conceive children, the Bible claims that Mary conceived "by the Spirit." I take that to mean that she conceived the child by hearing the Word of God, and that the Child was not conceived just because of fleshly concerns. He was conceived by the Spirit of God, not by the fleshly concerns of man. That is how the Bible sees her as the Mother of the Christ Child.

The necessity of seeing the nuturing, tender, supportive without-end side of God is very necessary in our time. We talk of Mother Church and Father God and we have totally confused the laity. Our image of God must encompass the best of both worlds, of both female and male, and

Greek Orthodox silver icon
of the Blessed Mother
From the author's collection

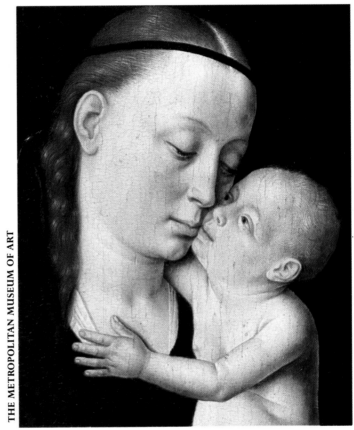

THE METROPOLITAN MUSEUM OF ART

"Virgin and Child," detail.
Dieric Bouts, Flemish,
active, 1457–1475

Russian Orthodox icon
of the Holy Mother
From the author's collection

thus I have come to a new appreciation of Mary as the Queen of Heaven. It is another way of talking about the serious affection, the unending love that God has for each of us.

And what are we to prepare for her in the manger? A salad of fresh greens and edible flowers, remembering that she is called the "Flower of Heaven."

A Flower Salad for Mary

Be careful when you choose the flowers for this dish. For instance, at Christmastime poinsettias are everywhere, but their leaves are poisonous. Choose flowers that have not been sprayed, and be sure that they are edible. Arugula flowers make a wonderful salad, as do any edible herb flowers that you may find. Roses are edible if they have not been sprayed, so are lovely calendulas. You also might find some Johnny-jump-ups, which look like little pansies. A good gourmet shop in any large city will have such a selection for you, usually all cleaned and sealed in a plastic bag.

Prepare a bed of tender greens and cover with the blossoms. Add a very light dressing and think of the coldness of that night in Bethlehem when Mary became known as the "Flower of Heaven."

The Baby Jesus

The cattle are lowing, the poor baby wakes,
But little Lord Jesus, no crying he makes.

I have trouble with this Christmas carol, just as I did when I was a child. Why did the Child not cry? Does the Bible imply that crying is a bad thing to do?

The whole meaning of the presence of the Child in the manger rests on our accepting the wonderful fact that God has come to be with us, as man and woman, and as we are. Of course the child cried, and I expect God continues to

cry over what we do to one another. How could it be otherwise? The One who has loved us to the point of degrading himself to be with us on humanly terms also must laugh a great deal. How could it be otherwise?

The people of that time were expecting a Messiah, one who would bring about the fulfillment of the Kingdom, one who would free them from the bondage of Rome, one who would restore the Temple to the significance that it deserved, one who would perhaps bring about the final event of the age. And they got a baby! God declares Himself/Herself as a baby. All of our images of power and might and takeovers are brought down by the Most High confessing Himself as a baby. Why should God confess Himself/Herself to us? The question astounds me, but the answer is plain. Because God chose to show us that love is stronger than anything that we have ever thought up in terms of power.

The feeling that each of us has when we see a baby is always the same: "He is so dependent upon me." Why would God say this to us? Because we are so dependent upon Him, and it is not a matter of power play . . . it is a matter of affection for us that is beyond our ability to believe

Nineteenth-century Spanish wood carving of the Christ Child From the author's collection, a gift from Craig, his chef

**Manger scene
From Jeff's crèche**

or understand. We are as dependent upon the Holy One as a tiny newborn child is dependent upon us. The fact that the Prince of Peace should declare Himself in this way is shocking, and just perfect, when you come to think about it.

What shall we prepare for the Child? Shhh . . . don't wake Him. We just got Him to sleep. But we can offer some milk and honey, remembering the promise given to our forefathers and foremothers that they would find fulfillment in the "land of milk and honey." It is hard for us to

understand how glorious that promise must have sounded to a people who had wandered and starved on the desert for so many years. A land where milk and honey FLOWS! That is a wonderful image of fulfillment, and the Child is our image of fulfillment.

**The Baby
From Jeff's crèche**

Milk and Honey for Jesus

MAKES 2 SERVINGS

This is simple to make and very delicious. Your kids will love it.

Place a pint of milk in a food blender and add 2 or 3 tablespoons of honey. (I usually warm my honey in the microwave for a moment so that it will blend well and be frothy. Leave the metal lid off the jar, of course.) Whip the mixture for just a moment and then pour into glasses and serve.

A Birthday Cake for Jesus

Your family might also wish to bake a birthday cake for Christmas Day dinner. Decorate it and invite all to the celebration of the birthday of the Prince of Peace.

Food typical of Biblical times:
a meal of dried fish, cheese, olives, bread,
salt, wine, and olive oil

Joseph,
The Carpenter

Joseph is a most interesting character in the manger scene, interesting in the sense that the poor man had so little to do. An angel explained to him that his betrothed, not yet his wife, was to bear a child and the child was to be called the Son of the Most High. Now Joseph, being a quiet and humble carpenter, certainly wondered why he was the one chosen to raise the Prince of Peace. From the Bible we hear about his questioning and consternation, but such did not last long. He watched over the birth of his child while in the manger, and watched over the raising of the boy until manhood.

Joseph, the Carpenter From Jeff's crèche

What should we prepare for Joseph? Something that a simple man would understand, such as unleavened brown bread cakes. You could make these and take them on a trip, as they would last a long time. We know that there were no inns that served food in those days, so the travelers brought their own supplies. When I told Craig, my assistant, this story, he yelled, "What, no room service in the manger?" No, there was no room service anywhere in town.

According to Ben Sirach, who wrote a great deal about the nature of the time and whose book is a part of the Apocrypha in the Bible, a normal meal probably consisted of flat bread, olives, olive oil and salt, wine, milk and honey, and, if it had been a good week, a bit of dried fish. Rarely did one eat red meat since the sheep had to function as milk givers, wool growers, and producers of an occasional baby lamb. Only on High Holy Days did one get a chance to eat meat. The above menu was much more common.

So, for Joseph in the manger the meal is unleavened brown bread, a common provision for the traveler at the time.

Unleavened Brown Bread for Joseph

MAKES 8 FLAT LOAVES

3 ½   cups whole-wheat flour

1   teaspoon salt

1 ¾   cups lukewarm water

  Additional flour for kneading

  Sesame oil for brushing

Combine the flour and salt in a large mixing bowl. Add the water and mix to form a dough. Place the dough on the counter and knead with additional flour until smooth and not sticky. Cover the dough with the large mixing bowl directly on the counter. Allow to rest for 2 hours. Cut the dough into 8 pieces and form into balls. Roll the dough balls into 8 circles on a lightly floured surface. Keep the dough covered with the bowl or plastic wrap when you are not working with it. Brush the flat loaves with a little sesame oil. The best method of cooking these is to bake them directly on baking tiles in a preheated 500° oven (the Saladay company manufactures such a product). Bake a few minutes until the edges curl up. You may also bake these on baking sheets.

"The Nativity," detail.
Gerard David, Flemish, active, 1484–1523

The Angels

On the night of the birth of the Child, Saint Luke records:

And in that region there were shepherds out in the field, keeping watch over their flock by night. And an angel of the Lord appeared to them, and the glory of the Lord shone around them, and they were filled with fear. And the angel said to them, "Be not afraid; for behold, I bring you good news of a great joy which will come to all people; for to you is born this day in the city of David a Savior, who is Christ the Lord. And this will be a sign for you: you will find a babe wrapped in swaddling cloths and lying in a manger." And suddenly there was with the angel a multitude of the heavenly host praising God and saying, "Glory to God in the Highest, and on earth peace among men with whom he is pleased."

"Angel," detail,
painted wood and terracotta,
various materials.
Gift of Loretta Hines Howard,
1964. Photograph by
Lee Boltin

"Abraham Feeding the Angels." Rembrandt.
Print from the author's collection

I am not sure whether or not I have been ᵥvisited by an angel, though I expect so . . . perhaps many times.

The word "angel" comes from the Biblical word for "messenger," *evangelium,* from which we get the word "evangelist" or "evangel." It means "the one who brings the good word."

In ancient times it was commonly believed that God could declare His word in any form at all, and so the wonderful messengers of the Bible, the evangelium or angels, usually assumed bodily form. I expect that that's about all we can understand.

Medieval artists usually portrayed the angels as being strictly feminine, though there is nothing in the Bible to support this. It probably had something to do with the feminine aspect of truth. Women, in my experience, are much quicker to see and know the truth than men. In any case, most of the more recent images of angels in art are feminine. However, I have found an etching by Rembrandt that shows Abraham preparing a meal for the angels. They had come to tell him that his elderly wife, Sarah, would be with child. And Abraham prepared a feast. Please note that in these images the angels do not look feminine at all but rather have receding hairlines and goatees. I like these images!

Now, since the angel appears at the manger, what shall He/She be fed? A dish of Angel Hair Pasta with Whipped Cream and Porcini (dried mushrooms), the perfect combination of the wheat of the earth, the mushrooms that grow from ruin, and whipped cream, which points to their clouds of travel. Honey Cake with Rose Water we will serve as a dessert, remembering the early Church blessing, "How sweet is your Word upon my lips!"

Angel Hair Pasta with Whipped Cream and Porcini

SERVES 4 TO 6

½ ounce dried porcini mushrooms

3 tablespoons olive oil

½ cup chopped shallots

¾ pound fresh mushrooms, chopped

½ pint (1 cup) whipping cream

¾ pound angel hair pasta

¼ cup grated Parmesan cheese

   Salt and freshly ground black pepper to taste

Place the porcini in a small bowl and add ½ cup warm water. Allow to soak 45 minutes. Drain, reserving the liquid. Heat a large frying pan. Add the oil and shallots, and sauté a minute. Add the fresh mushrooms and sauté until tender. Chop the porcini coarsely and add to the frying pan, along with the reserved liquid. Simmer until most of the liquid is evaporated.

Bring a large pot of water to a boil along with a pinch of salt. In a separate bowl, whip the cream until it holds soft peaks. Refrigerate the whipped cream until the pasta is cooked. Cook the pasta in the boiling water until *al dente.* Drain well. Return the drained pasta to the pot and add the mushroom mixture, cheese, whipped cream, and salt and pepper to taste.

Using a large spatula, fold all of the ingredients together. Do this quickly, yet carefully, so that the whipped cream doesn't collapse entirely. You may want to save a bit of the whipped cream to dollop on top of the pasta as a garnish. Serve immediately.

I think this is a very clever dish, and I can say that because I did not invent it. Craig, my cook, and I agreed that angel hair pasta would be fine for the angels, but he came up with this wonderful marriage of mushrooms and clouds. Incidentally, you don't have to buy the very expensive dried Italian porcini. You can find dried mushrooms from South America that are much cheaper, and they are very good. Enjoy this dish and think of the wonderful bond that the Bible makes between Heaven and Earth.

The following recipe is simply the wonderful honey cake given us by Fanny Silverstein, author of My Mother's Cookbook, a recipe that I published in a previous book. We have substituted rose water for the brandy called for in Fanny's Honey Cake. Rose water would be much more familiar to the angels than brandy, don't you think? It is a delightful change, and it tastes very Middle Eastern.

Honey Cake with Rose Water for the Angels

SERVES 12

3	cups all-purpose flour
1 ½	teaspoons baking powder
¼	teaspoon ground cinnamon
½	teaspoon baking soda
1	tablespoon instant coffee
½	cup boiling water
¼	cup vegetable oil or peanut oil
1	cup honey
	Grated peel of 1 orange
2	teaspoons rose water (find in Greek markets)
4	eggs
1	cup sugar
1	cup chopped walnuts

Combine the flour, baking powder, cinnamon, and baking soda. Set aside. Dissolve the instant coffee in the water in a mixing bowl. Blend in the oil, honey, grated orange peel, and rose water and set aside. In a large bowl, beat the eggs until frothy. Gradually add the sugar and beat for 1 minute. Add the honey mixture to the eggs and sugar. Add the flour mixture to the egg mixture alternately with the dissolved coffee, starting and ending with the dry ingredients. Stir in the walnuts. Pour the batter into an oiled and waxed paper-lined 13 by 9 by 2-inch baking pan. Bake in a preheated 325° oven for about 50 minutes. Test for doneness with a toothpick. If moist, continue baking until a toothpick inserted in the center comes out clean. Invert the cake onto a wire rack. Cool. Peel off the waxed paper and wrap in aluminum foil to maintain freshness. Cut into squares when ready to serve.

"The Nativity," detail.
Antoniazzo Romano, Roman, active, 1461–1508

The Shepherds

"While shepherds watched their flocks by night" the world changed about them. The shepherds really did not own their flocks, you know, as the sheep were owned by many members and families of the community. The shepherds were simply to take care of the sheep, not own them.

Is it not interesting that we have a single word for sheep? It is the same word whether you are talking about one sheep or a hundred sheep, since sheep are totally communal in their life-style, just as we are supposed to be.

The life of the shepherd was probably not very exciting in Biblical times, but he did learn a lot about living in a community. For instance, he learned that sheep must be together. Separate and part them from the flock and they will die. Just die. The Bible claims that we are the same. We need each other. Further, the shepherd learned that when a ewe, a momma sheep, gives birth to a lamb and the lamb dies, the momma is devastated with grief and she herself may die of the pain. The keeper of the flock also learned that if he were to put a mother who has lost her lamb during birth with an orphan born during the night, the two would not accept one another. The grieving mother would thus die of a broken heart, and the tiny orphan, born of some other ewe, would die from lack of sustenance. The Biblical writers understood this desert image because they were of the desert, and everyone, everyone, understood the images of the desert when the Bible was written. The only way that a shepherd could save the life of the orphaned lamb sounds strange to us, since we know nothing of the desert ethic. The shepherd had to slit the throat of the dead baby, the child of the grieving mother, and rub the body of the orphaned lamb in the dead lamb's blood. Then the mother,

even in the midst of her grieving, would smell her own and she would immediately adopt the orphan, even though he was foreign to her, and he did not belong to her. Nevertheless, the momma would move so that the lamb that she smelled could come and suckle. He could come home to the feast, though he did not belong.

The Bible claims that Jesus was as a sheep who died and His blood was offered as a symbol of our adoption by the Holy One: We certainly do not deserve to come home to the table . . . but the image of Jesus as Shepherd is basic to Biblical theology, and it is an image that I cherish and love. So, the shepherd must be present at the birth. He was one of the most profound theologians present at the manger.

**Shepherd
From Jeff's crèche**

Now, as to the "Hillside." Can you imagine the fear and awe of the shepherds when the angel came upon them and announced the birth of the Prince of Peace? The shepherds were minding their own business, keeping watch over the flocks by night. "Look out for dogs and thieves." Then it happened! The fire was low; all heads were nodding in and out of a mild slumber. Suddenly, the angel appeared and told the shepherds that all things would be different

since a child had been born, the Son of the Most High. "And you will find the child dressed in swaddling cloths and lying in a manger." What an announcement! Surely they were confused, and the sense of awe we can understand. But, they went and found the child, and, like you and I, did not fully comprehend. But, they fell down and worshipped Him, just as you and I.

What shall we prepare for the shepherds? Roast lamb would be a natural, would it not? But please remember that red meat was served only on High Holy Days. The rest of the time the shepherd would have lived on a diet more customary in his time. The common meal probably would have been bread dipped in wine, and a soup made with olives. Dipping bread in wine, by the way, is a great way of enjoying bread without using butter or (ugh!) margarine.

Bread in Wine
for the Shepherd Boy

It seems hardly necessary to describe this dish, since the title alone should do it for you. Rather than using butter or oil on your bread, simply dip crusty French bread into a good red wine. This would have been common in the ancient world, and given our fear of calories, it should become common in our time.

**Shepherd Boy
From Jeff's crèche**

Green Olive Soup
for the Shepherd Boy

SERVES 6 TO 8

2 cups pitted green olives

3 tablespoons olive oil

½ medium yellow onion, peeled and sliced

2 cloves garlic, peeled and crushed

4 cups Chicken Stock (page 275)

1 cup whipping cream

3 tablespoons olive oil

6 tablespoons all-purpose flour

Freshly ground black pepper to taste (no salt will be necessary due to the olives)

4 shots Tabasco

⅓ cup dry sherry

Garnish

Sliced pimiento-stuffed green olives

Garlic bread croutons

Soak the green olives in cold water for 1 hour. Drain and coarsely chop. Heat a frying pan and add 3 tablespoons of the olive oil, the onion, and garlic, along with two thirds of the olives. Sauté until the onion is transparent. Purée the mixture in a food processor with 1 cup of the chicken stock.

In a 4-quart saucepan, combine the purée mixture with the remaining stock. Simmer for 20 minutes and add the cream. In a small frying pan, cook the remaining 3 table-spoons olive oil and the flour together to form a roux. Whisk the roux into the soup and simmer, stirring constantly, until thickened. Add black pepper to taste, the remaining chopped olives, the Tabasco, and sherry. Heat to serving temperature and serve with the sliced olive and crouton garnish.

The Sheep

Sheep must be at the manger scene, of course. After all, the Gospel of Saint John calls Jesus "the Good Shepherd" and claims that we are all like sheep and need a shepherd. What could that possibly mean?

First of all, sheep are not very smart. As a matter of fact, they are very dumb. If sheep are not cared for, they will wander off into the most disastrous situations. The line about sheep being led to slaughter is quite sound since sheep will follow the leader anywhere . . . anywhere at all. We need a shepherd or we will be lost.

The wonderful Christmas carol that sings about "Sheep on the hillside lay, whiter than snow," was written by a person who must never have seen sheep on a hillside. They are anything but "whiter than snow." To be truthful, they are filthy. Just filthy! Why am I telling you this? No, I am not trying to destroy Christmas legend or mythology, but unless you understand that sheep are quite stupid and dirty you will never understand why Jesus is referred to as the Good Shepherd.

The early traditions, the Old Testament, talk of a Messiah who would come and care for us like a shepherd, and feed the flocks. The term *pastor* in the Church comes from the "feeding" task of the clergy, going out to pasture with the sheep. Further, Saint John claims that Jesus knows the name of each of his flock and would not hesitate to leave ninety-nine sheep in the fold to go out and search for a single sheep that is lost. What kind of a shepherd is that? Certainly not a good businessman . . . but rather the image of the Child of Christmas grown to be a shepherd of all of the sheep, every one. John even claims that Jesus as the Good Shepherd would lay down his life for his sheep. Such a beautiful image of the life of the Messiah.

Of course sheep must be present at the manger scene. After all, the manger is not just to show what was happening at the time, but it is also to show what will happen in the future.

We need the sheep in our manger.

Sheep
From Jeff's crèche

What will we feed them? I think they would like a nice green salad. A little light on the dressing, of course, but a salad made of the fresh greens that you and I can buy in our time—such wonderfully fresh greens. In the old days in Bethlehem the sheep would have had to be content with rather dry grasses and desert vegetation that would be a far cry from what we could offer them today. So, for the sheep, a great green salad! Be sure to add some onions, garlic, leeks, and cucumbers—favorite foods during Biblical times.

The Cattle

The term *cattle* in the Bible is used to describe several animals, even goats, but it generally refers to a beef cow or an ox. It was necessary to have such creatures, even in a poor house, in ancient Jerusalem since they were beasts of burden and did work in the fields. Rarely were they eaten, though there are Biblical stories of the very wealthy people, those who owned several or a herd of such animals, eating them on special occasions.

We have to remember that red meat was eaten only on High Holy Days in Biblical times, and then it was usually lamb or goat. Chickens were not known in Palestine, a thought that is difficult for us to imagine.

It took me a while to discover what the term "lowing" means, as in "The Cattle are Lowing." I was expecting some marvelous theological insight, but I came up with "mooing." "To low" is "to moo," from an ancient word for "calling." I decided the cattle were mooing when the little child was born. Then two dear friends of mine heard of my plight and called me. One, Michael Self, a fine tenor who should know nothing about animals, explained that lowing was the sound the animal made late in the evening, and it was not a moo at all—just a low sort of sound. The second friend, Ron Fields, who holds a Ph.D. in art history, called and offered his advice. What does a Ph.D. in art history know about cattle in the shed? He was raised in the hills of Arkansas and he knew his chores as a child. "At the end of the day, when it begins to darken, the mother is filled with milk and calls her child to come and suckle. The sound that she makes at that time of day is called lowing. It is not a moo at all." There I had it! The sound that a mother makes when calling her child is that of lowing . . . and "The cattle are lowing, the poor baby wakes." Again we see the blessing of the feminine side of God as the nurturer, and the Blessed Mother Mary was there to suckle her child.

Now, what do we feed the cattle? Their normal diet

Cow
From Jeff's crèche

was simply whatever grass they could locate and dry straw in the winter, the same diet that cattle eat in our time. But, since barley was so common at the time, and since I am sure that the cattle would love some grain, I offer them—and you—a barley casserole. This is an old but very delicious dish.

Baked Barley Casserole for the Cattle

SERVES 4 TO 6

1   cup barley
     Butter
3   tablespoons olive oil or peanut oil
2 or 3   medium yellow onions, peeled and chopped
     Salt and freshly ground black pepper to taste
6   cups chicken or beef broth *

Brown the barley in a little butter and the oil. Place in a casserole. Brown the yellow onions in butter, and add them to the barley. Add salt and pepper. Add 3 cups of the chicken or beef broth, cover, and place in a 350° oven for about 1 hour, or until the moisture is almost absorbed. Add another 3 cups of broth, and cook, covered, until absorbed. (Yes, that is right: 1 cup barley to 6 cups broth.)

*If you use your own Beef Stock, made according to the directions on page 274, you need to use less stock and more water; your homemade stock is so rich in gelatin that water must be added so that the barley will cook properly. So, if you use homemade stock for this recipe, use 4 cups of stock and 2 cups of water instead of the 6 cups stock called for.

I know that you would not serve a cow a cooked casserole, but since we rarely eat uncooked grain, and since barley would have been a special treat for cattle in Biblical times, we will cook a barley casserole.

The Donkey

The donkey was standing in the manger, watching the birth. Oh, all right, he was probably an ass, the ancestor of what we call the donkey. In any case, this donkey, or ass, was not very smart. As a matter of fact he was, and remains, a rather dumb and stubborn farm animal that is used most usually by those who can afford little else in terms of farm help. He is an animal of low, low estate.

Why is he in the manger scene? It is because this animal of low estate, this common and lowly animal, carried Jesus into town on Palm Sunday. It is very important to remember that all of the animals at the manger scene had something to do with the future. Well, the donkey had his

Donkey
From Jeff's crèche

time, but it was a degrading time. That seems to be what the donkey is for, in terms of the Biblical story.

During Palm Sunday we celebrate the entrance of Jesus into Jerusalem. You must understand that the people of this city were expecting a very exciting Messiah, one who would free them from the captivity of their Roman invaders. They looked to Jesus to be that strong conqueror who would lead them in the great battle to free the people of Israel from bondage to the Caesars of Rome. One day it was announced that the Messiah was coming into Jerusalem and all prepared to meet Him. Palm branches were cut and were to be waved about the coming conqueror, and a great celebration was to be had. But Jesus, deciding that war is not the route to peace and fulfillment, told his followers to find him a donkey. Jesus rode into the cheering crowd on a donkey! Noth-

ing in the Old World was lower than a donkey, nothing. How confused these people must have been when they were expecting a great and powerful warrior and saw instead the Prophet riding on a poor old donkey. The shock is close to that of the manger scene, very close indeed.

We still do not seem to understand that the King of the Universe expects us to seek peace by riding the donkey rather than the images of power and might. I hope we learn very soon!

Now, since we need the donkey at the manger, what shall he be fed? He will eat "Straw and Hay," one of the best pasta dishes that I know.

The name for this colorful pasta dish comes from the fact that you use pasta of two different colors, yellow and green. Straw and Hay is the rich-tasting result.

Straw and Hay
Paglia e Fieno

SERVES 6 AS A PASTA COURSE

½   cup (1 stick) butter
¼   cup olive oil
4   cloves garlic, peeled and minced
½   pound spinach linguine
½   pound regular linguine
⅓   cup grated Parmesan cheese
Salt and freshly ground black pepper to taste
Additional cheese for topping

Heat a small frying pan and add the butter, olive oil, and garlic. Sauté the garlic briefly, but do not burn. Set aside. Bring a large pot of water with a pinch of salt to a boil and in it cook both pastas. (Check the cooking times for both types of pasta so that you can time them properly.) Drain. Return the pasta to the pot and toss with the reserved butter and garlic mixture, the cheese, and salt and pepper to taste. To serve, top the individual portions with additional cheese.

The Innkeeper

We must not forget the innkeeper. I think he has gotten a bum rap through the years, and he comes off in our tradition as being rather unkind, putting Mary and Joseph out in the back shed when he saw she was pregnant. But, after all, he had no rooms left. The town was packed with people who had to come to register for the Roman taxes, and he did the most thoughtful thing he could. He said, "Well, I have no place for you here, but I'll let you sleep with the cattle. It should not be too cold with all those animals around."

You see, he was probably a rather kind man after all. What shall we prepare for him? I suspect that he and his

wife ate a lot of soup. The inn had no dining room, and meals were not served, but I am sure that he had some soup in his own kitchen that he would offer a hungry guest on occasion. So, for the innkeeper a good soup.

The Innkeeper
From Jeff's crèche

Barley Soup
for the Innkeeper

SERVES 6

8   cups Chicken Stock (page 275)

1   medium yellow onion, peeled and sliced

1   cup chopped celery with leaves

2   cloves garlic, peeled and crushed

1   cup cleaned and chopped leeks

¾   cup pearl barley

2   cups cold water

3   tablespoons chopped fresh parsley

2   tablespoons chopped fresh coriander

½   teaspoon ground cumin

   Salt and freshly ground black pepper to taste

In a 6-quart pot, place the chicken stock, onion, celery, garlic, and leeks. Bring to a boil and simmer, covered, until the vegetables are tender, about 20 minutes. Combine the barley and the water in a small saucepan. Bring to a boil and simmer, covered, 10 minutes. Drain the barley and add to the pot of vegetables and stock. Simmer, covered, another 20 minutes. Add the parsley, coriander, and cumin, and simmer, uncovered, for 10 minutes, or longer for a thicker soup. Salt and pepper to taste.

Barley was a very common grain at the time of the Birth. It makes a wonderful and inexpensive soup since it swells up to three times its original size.

The Tax Collector

We know that the tax collector was hanging around the manger. After all, that is why Joseph and Mary went to Bethlehem—to pay their taxes to Rome.

Now we must understand that the tax collectors were hired by the Romans to collect taxes from the Jews. The money they collected was then sent to Rome and used to pay the soldiers to keep the Jews in captivity. Put yourself in the Jewish people's place and you will immediately become very angry. Further, this tax collector was a fellow Jew, this character who added a surcharge to your taxes for himself, claiming some sort of personal overhead. He was not a popular man. Zacchius was a tax collector, and you

will remember that he had to climb up a tree to see Jesus preaching because no one in the crowd would let him in. Not popular at all!

Popularity sometimes has nothing to do with wealth since the tax collectors did very well for themselves. For dinner with this man, even though you would not like to feed him, I suggest some wonderful lamb chops pan-roasted and served with onions sautéed with yogurt and sesame oil.

Pan-Roasted Lamb Chops for the Tax Collector

SERVES 4

8   loin lamb chops, double cut, about 2 inches thick
    Salt and freshly ground black pepper to taste
1   tablespoon olive oil

Preheat the oven to 400°. Season the lamb with salt and pepper. Heat a large ovenproof frying pan and add the oil. Brown the chops quickly over medium-high heat. Place the whole pan with the lamb in the oven. Roast the lamb chops 2 minutes per side for medium rare. After 4 minutes in the

Can you imagine the cost of thick lamb chops in the ancient world? We can barely afford them now, and prices for food in our time are much lower, per capita income, than was food in earlier times. Make them anyhow. Just be sure that the tax collector, should

oven, remove the pan and set the frying pan in a warm place and allow the meat to rest in the pan another 2 minutes. This will relax the meat and finish the cooking. Serve with Onions Sautéed with Yogurt and Sesame Oil (below).

Onions Sautéed with Yogurt and Sesame Oil

SERVES 6 TO 8 AS A SIDE DISH

4   tablespoons olive oil
5   medium yellow onions, peeled and sliced
1   pint yogurt
2   tablespoons chopped fresh parsley
2   tablespoons sesame oil
    Salt and freshly ground black pepper to taste

Heat a large frying pan and add the olive oil and onions. Sauté for 3 minutes, then reduce the heat to low. Cover and cook for 5 minutes to "sweat" the onions down. Remove the lid and finish sautéing the onions until tender. Do not brown too much. Stir in the yogurt and warm a minute until smooth. Stir in the parsley, sesame oil, and salt and pepper to taste.

he appear at your Christmas table, eats by himself.

When Craig, my cook, and I developed this dish, I smiled and said, "Bible!" He did not have to ask me what I meant because this dish tastes like food must have tasted in Biblical times. Onions, yogurt, and sesame oil were common food products, but this dish is rich enough for some misled tax collector.

The
Roman Troops

It is very hard to imagine how the peoples of Israel felt about the Roman soldiers who were always present. In America we have never seen occupation troops, but they were common throughout the life of Jesus. They were hated and considered outsiders. But it was the custom of the time to feed even one's enemies, so, in the spirit of Christmas, we shall consider a meal for the Roman soldiers.

Please remember that these fellows had eaten very well when at home in Rome, the greatest city of its time. Good

food was readily available and of enormous variety. The Romans have always loved to eat . . . and they still do! They believed in ancient times that the troops were to eat well, and thus they were fed well.

When these same troops went off to conquer Egypt, they also ate very well. Because the Nile river floods the fields each year, bringing new silt and nutrition to the soil, farming in Egypt was very productive. One writer of the time said that all you had to do was to put a seed in the ground and stand back. Thus the diet that was offered to the soldiers in Egypt was fresh, varied, and delicious. The Egyptians were great bread bakers and they loved vegetables of every variety.

Can you imagine how these same troops, accustomed to really good eating, must have reacted when they hit Palestine? Their menu was cut back due to the slim list of foodstuffs available to the normal Jew. Their love of vegetables had to be satisfied by leeks, onions, beans, and lentils. No wonder these troops were always in such a bad mood! Jesus tells his followers that if a Roman soldier suddenly grabbed you and demanded that you carry his bag a mile (a common occurrence at the time), you were to carry it two

miles and thus confound the poor fellow. No, the Roman troops were not a friendly lot.

For dinner with the soldiers, we must remember that we are to feed even the enemy. That is the law in the Bible. So I have prepared a dish of vegetables and grains, a dish that the troops would love. I have included cucumbers in the dish because the troops missed them so since leaving Egypt. Today in Rome this dish would still be very popular.

Grains with Vegetables for the Roman Troops

SERVES 10

1   cup pearl barley
7   cups Chicken Stock (page 275)
1   cup lentils
1   cup coarse-grain bulgur wheat
4   tablespoons olive oil
1   large yellow onion, peeled and sliced
2   cups cleaned and coarsely chopped leeks
2   cucumbers, peeled and coarsely chopped
½   cup chopped fresh parsley
    Salt and freshly ground black pepper to taste

In a 6- to 8-quart pot, simmer the barley in 3 cups of the chicken stock, covered, for 30 minutes. Add the lentils and 2 more cups stock. Simmer for 15 minutes. Add the bulgur and the remaining 2 cups of stock. Cook for 20 minutes.

Heat a large frying pan and add the olive oil, onion, and leeks and sauté until just tender. Stir the sautéed vege-

The Roman troops loved grains and must be credited with the popularization of all kinds of polentas. The use of three different grains in one dish would have been appreciated by the Roman boys.

tables into the pot with the cucumbers and parsley. Simmer gently, covered, for an additional 10 minutes. Salt and pepper to taste.

The Beggar

There must have been a beggar at the manger scene. I expect that poverty and begging were even more common in Biblical times than in our own, so we know that a beggar was present.

The early traditions, the Old Testament, had several laws pertaining to one's responsibility to the needy and homeless. If you owned an orchard or farm, you were to leave the corners unharvested so that those wandering the road might stop and eat from your field. Certain amounts of money were to be given to the poor, and almsgiving was

widely practiced. This gives us some indication of the size of the problem.

Finally, the beggar must be present at the scene because years later, in the great Sermon on the Mount called the Beatitudes, Jesus claims that the hungry, the meek, and the poor in spirit will be satisfied, comforted, and see the Kingdom of God.

I remember as a child, during World War II, how my mother would feed the hungry on our porch. Dad was at work, and I would see a poor and dirty fellow come to our door. He would ask for food, and my mother always responded, though the guest was expected to eat on the steps, not in the house. Since I knew that she had trouble enough already making ends meet, I asked her why she always fed these fellows. She quietly replied, "Nobody should be hungry." She was right, of course.

This Christmas you might think of a special gift for those who are hungry. Your local food bank will be drained by Christmas morning, and it would be great if your family were to deliver a check to the food distributor just when it needs it most. Or, I have suggested in the past that you buy a calf through the Heifer Project (Heifer Project International, P.O. Box 808, Little Rock, Arkansas 72203;

501-376-6836 or 800-422-0474) and have it shipped to a family in some poverty-stricken nation. It would provide the family with milk, and perhaps a small dairy herd could be established. No, the cow would not be eaten. Or perhaps you might choose to send a goat, which could provide milk, cheese, and clothing.

I recently wrote the following letter to a church:

To my friends at First United Methodist Church in Ocala, Florida

How pleased I am to hear that you are continuing to support the Heifer Project International. How wonderful it would be if your families were to each decide to send an animal of some sort to poverty-stricken peoples. I suggest you send the check to the Heifer Project and then wrap up a package and put it under your tree. Mark the tag to your family, and on Christmas morning open it up. Inside have a note concerning your gift and then just try to imagine how excited the actual recipients would be. It is more important than the kind of Christmas gifts that you and I normally give one another.

I bid you Peace, especially during this blessed season.

You might also consider giving a check to AmeriCare, an agency that I trust. The address is 161 Cherry Street, New Canaan, Connecticut 06840. Be sure to have each of your children sign the card so that they might understand the funds are coming from the whole family.

What meal shall we prepare for the beggar? His normal meal would probably consist of bread and sop, or gravy. I remember my father eating bread with gravy on it, and I remember how he used to tell me that this was one of the common dishes of his childhood. As he grew older and did not have to eat such a thing, he began to miss the dish. So, in the memory of the beggar at the manger, try putting torn-up bread in a bowl. Top it with a good brown gravy and eat. It is typical of the meal that many destitute people eat often. And remember my mother's line: "No one should be hungry."

Gravy for
Dipping and Sopping

MAKES ABOUT 4 CUPS

2 ½   cups Beef Stock (page 274)

¼   cup dry red wine

4   tablespoons (½ stick) butter

½   cup all-purpose flour

2   tablespoons olive oil

1   medium yellow onion, peeled and sliced

1   tablespoon Maggi Liquid Seasoning (find in the grocery store)

  Salt and freshly ground black pepper to taste

  Pita bread

In small saucepan, bring the beef stock and wine to a simmer. Melt the butter in a small frying pan and add the flour. Cook together to form a roux. Add the roux to the hot stock mixture and whisk it in with a wire whisk. Simmer the gravy, whipping it until smooth and lump free.

Heat a frying pan and add the olive oil and the onion. Sauté until transparent. Add to the gravy with the Maggi and the salt and pepper to taste. Serve over the pita bread torn into pieces.

I know that the term "sop" probably does not appeal to you, but people ate it all the time in ancient times. It appears to be the last meal that Jesus ate, in the Upper Room, when he dipped bread in sop and offered it to Judas.

The Epiphany
and the Three
Wise Men

Advent is the season of the preparation for the coming of the Child, a season that begins on the fourth Sunday before Christmas. It is followed by the Feast of Christmas, which lasts for twelve days, though most of us rarely celebrate the whole season. Finally comes the Epiphany, the season of the recognition of Jesus as the Prince of Peace, the Son of the Most High, the Messiah. Beginning on January 6, the season lasts until Ash Wednesday. It is that time of the year in which recognition is celebrated from peoples all over the earth, and thus it is the season of the

Three Wise Men who came from the East, saying, "Where is He who is born King of the Jews, for we have seen His star in the East, and have come to worship Him."

Who were these three men from the East? Only Saint Matthew tells of their visit, and they are not mentioned again anywhere in the New Testament. Matthew's description of the visit does not call them kings but rather Magi, a word that refers to wise scholars who were probably astrologers. The sign of the star had been predicted, and thus they came seeking the predicted birth of a king, though they were probably not kings themselves. Following the star, they came and found the Child, and fell down and worshipped Him.

The gifts the Magi brought that Saint Matthew mentions are significant for their symbolism in the Old World, and beautiful in their meaning for our time. One of the wise men brought a gift of gold, the kind of gift that would have been given to a King. The second brought a incense burner filled with frankincense, the very kind of incense that would be used in the service of worship for the Most High. The third wise man brought a gift of myrrh, a balm used in healing, as a perfume, and in the preparation of a dead body

**Wise Man with myrrh
From Jeff's crèche**

**Wise Man with gold
From Jeff's crèche**

for burial. Behold, the wise men bring the three things that foretell the life of the Baby, the role of Son of God, the expected Messiah, and the eventual death on the Cross.

Later traditions claimed that the three were actually kings, but the Bible never mentions same. We can assume that they came from Persia, or perhaps what is now Saudi Arabia, since that is the place where the myrrh would have been found. In any case, they came expecting to find an incredible event. There actually was a conjunction of Jupiter and Saturn in the constellation of Pisces that would have produced a great light, the expected star, around the time of the birth of the Child of Bethlehem. The wise men knew from ancient traditions that such a sign in the heavens would indicate the birth of a most powerful and significant person, and thus they followed the star . . . and found a baby in very low estate.

Wise Man with frankincense From Jeff's crèche

The shock that the wise men must have felt is, for me, one of the most fascinating things about the manger scene. They certainly did not find the great leader and warrior that they were expecting. They found instead a symbol of very quiet and powerful love and peace . . . and I expect that it changed their lives.

T. S. Eliot, a favorite poet of mine, was also a fine theologian. When he contemplated the feelings that the wise men must have had upon finding the Baby, he decided that they must have felt not at all wise, but rather like fools. Saint Paul says in I Corinthians that the appearance of God in the form of a Baby made foolish all of the wisdom of the world. Our rational approach to understanding God has gotten us nowhere; thus our wisdom has been turned to foolishness so that we might understand the love of the Holy One.

I should stop. Eliot does not need my explanations, as you will see in his wonderful poem "Journey of the Magi." The poem is terribly profound and deals with the feelings that one of the wealthy magi had upon meeting the Child. He was so changed by the visit that he felt he had suffered a death of his old self, and thus became disturbed by his old life. Have your family read this together several times . . . so that it will become yours. It is filled with symbols for that which was to mark the life of Jesus.

Journey of the Magi
T. S. Eliot

"A cold coming we had of it,

Just the worst time of the year

For a journey, and such a long journey:

The ways deep and the weather sharp,

The very dead of winter."

And the camels galled, sore-footed, refractory,

Lying down in the melted snow.

There were times we regretted

The summer palaces on slopes, the terraces,

And the silken girls bringing sherbet.

Then the camel men cursing and grumbling

And running away, and wanting their liquor
    and women,

And the night-fires going out, and the lack of shelters,

And the cities hostile and the towns unfriendly

And the villages dirty and charging high prices:

A hard time we had of it.

At the end we preferred to travel all night,

Sleeping in snatches,

With the voices ringing in our ears, saying
That this was all folly.

Then at dawn we came down to a temperate valley,
Wet, below the snow line, smelling of vegetation;
With a stream running and a water-mill beating
        the darkness,
And three trees on the low sky,
And an old white horse galloped away in the meadow.
Then we came to a tavern with vine-leaves over the lintel,
Six hands at an open door dicing for pieces of silver,
And feet kicking the empty wine-skins.
But there was no information, and so we continued
And arrived at evening, not a moment too soon
Finding the place; it was (you may say) satisfactory.
All this was a long time ago, I remember,
And I would do it again, but set down
This set down
This: were we led all that way for
Birth or Death? There was a Birth, certainly,
We had evidence and no doubt. I had seen birth
        and death,

But had thought they were different; this Birth was

Hard and bitter agony for us, like Death, our death.

We returned to our places, these Kingdoms,

But no longer at ease here, in the old dispensation,

With an alien people clutching their gods.

I should be glad of another death.

Three Kings and attendants.
Painted wood and terracotta, various materials.
Gift of Loretta Hines Howard, 1964.
Photograph by Museum Photo. Studio.

For each of the Magi we need a dish. And these dishes must be rich with the flavors and the wealth of ancient Persia and Arabia. A wine filled with the flavors of roses would have been a common delight for such a scholar, as would Lamb Meatballs, Persian Style. Finally, a rich Currant Cake with Rose Water should keep the three happy.

Three Wise Men
From Jeff's crèche

Rose Wine

MAKES ABOUT 1 QUART

1 bottle dry red wine
½ cup rose jam

Mix together both ingredients well and refrigerate in a glass container, covered, for 2 days. Strain, bring to room temperature, and serve.

  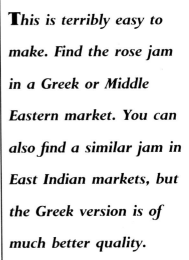

This is terribly easy to make. Find the rose jam in a Greek or Middle Eastern market. You can also find a similar jam in East Indian markets, but the Greek version is of much better quality.

A DISH FOR EACH
OF THE MAGI

Rose Wine

**Lamb Meatballs,
Persian Style**

**Currant Cake with
Rose Water**

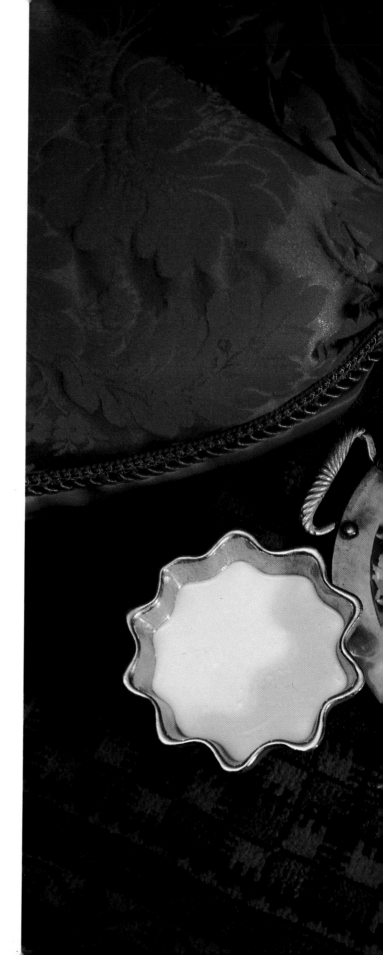

Lamb Meatballs, Persian Style

SERVES 6 TO 8

This takes a little doing, but get the kids involved forming the meatballs and have them think about how a Persian wise man or astrologer would have eaten such things regularly, and the old boys must have loved them.

¾ cup fine ground bulgur wheat

2 cups boiling water

The Meatballs

2 pounds lamb stew meat, ground fine

½ cup finely chopped yellow onion

½ cup pine nuts

3 tablespoons olive oil

2 eggs, beaten

1 teaspoon ground coriander

2 teaspoons ground cumin

3 tablespoons lemon juice

2 tablespoons chopped fresh dill

1 tablespoon chopped fresh mint

½ teaspoon salt

Freshly ground black pepper to taste

In a small bowl, allow the bulgur to soak in the boiling water ½ hour. Drain well.

In a large bowl, combine the meatball ingredients, including the drained bulgur, and mix very well. Form into 1½-inch balls and place on a baking sheet. (Keep your hands damp with a little water to facilitate forming the meatballs.) Bake 20 minutes in a preheated 375° oven, or until just cooked through.

The Sauce

2   tablespoons olive oil

1   medium yellow onion, peeled and sliced

2. pints yogurt

4   tablespoons cornstarch

2   tablespoons cold water

    Salt to taste

Heat a frying pan and add the oil and the onion. Sauté until tender but do not brown. In a small saucepan, heat the yogurt to a gentle simmer, stirring regularly. Mix the cornstarch and water together until lump free. Whisk the cornstarch mixture into the heated yogurt, and stir until smooth and thickened. Add the sautéed onion and salt to taste to the yogurt. Set the sauce aside and keep warm.

The Rice

1½   cups Basmati rice

3   cups water

1   teaspoon salt, or to taste

In a small pot, bring the rice, water, and salt to a boil. Cover and simmer 15 minutes.

Garnish

    Sumac (Herb grown in the Middle East. Burgundy or rust in color and has a wonderful, tangy flavor.) to taste

    Chopped fresh parsley

To serve, spread the rice over a large platter. Top with the meatballs and the sauce. Garnish with the sumac and chopped parsley.

Currant Cake
with Rose Water

MAKES 3 CAKES

Rose water was used to flavor many things in the ancient world. You can find this rose extract in any good gourmet shop. Buy the kind from France, not from the Middle East.

The Batter

1   cup (2 sticks) butter, at room temperature

1   cup sugar

2   eggs, at room temperature

1   teaspoon vanilla

2   cups currants

3   cups applesauce

½   teaspoon salt

1   teaspoon ground cinnamon

½   teaspoon ground cloves

1   tablespoon baking soda

4   cups all-purpose flour

Cream the butter and sugar together until fluffy (I use my KitchenAid mixer). Add the eggs and vanilla and beat until smooth. Add the remaining ingredients for the batter and beat again. Grease 3 loaf pans, 8¼ × 4½ × 3 inches each. Divide the batter among the pans. Bake in a 300° oven for 1 hour, or until a toothpick inserted in the center comes out clean. Remove the pans to a cooling rack.

The Syrup

¼   cup honey

¾   cup sugar

¾   cup water

3   whole cloves

1   ½-inch piece cinnamon stick

1   tablespoon rose water (find in Greek markets)

Combine the ingredients for the syrup, except the rose water, in a small saucepan. Heat until the sugar dissolves. Add
the rose water.

To finish, pour the hot syrup over the warm cakes in
their pans. Allow to soak in and cool. Unmold on a rack,
slice, and serve.

The Camel

The camel, the great ship of the desert, appears in the manger scene not because he would have been regularly seen in Bethlehem, for such a beast was not used much by the peoples of Palestine. The camel is present in the crèche because of the Wise Men from the East.

In the very early days of the Bible camels seem to have been more common with the people of Israel. Abraham was said to have had several camels, and Jacob sent camels to his brother, Esau. That was about four thousand years ago. The creatures were used for travel, for bearing heavy bur-

Camel and camel driver
From Jeff's crèche

dens, and for wool. Saint John the Baptist came in from the desert wearing a cloak of camel wool. Finally, some peoples in the Middle East ate camel. My wife, Patty, who lived in the Middle East as a child, tasted the meat in Saudi Arabia. However, the Jews would never eat camel or drink their milk because the animal does not have a cloven hoof, thus making its use as a food a violation of kosher law.

Since the camel is the largest animal that would have been found in the desert, Jesus creates a wonderful hyperbole when he claims that "It is easier for a camel to walk through the eye of a needle than it is for a rich man (self-centered and selfish) to enter the Kingdom of Heaven."

So the camel appears at the manger, foretelling the preaching ministry of Jesus. The New Testament does not actually say that the wise men came by camel, but I expect that tradition has made a very good guess.

What should we feed the ship of the desert? He would eat grass, beans, or barley, and now and then the camel boy would give the creature some dates. So, let's put a bowl of dates on the table and remember the camel.

CHRISTMAS TRADITIONS

Santa Claus

I remember clearly the growing suspicion that I held each Christmas as a child . . . a suspicion that I did not really understand the Santa Claus thing. As I grew older I claimed to be very sophisticated and thus a disbeliever.

Now, I wish to return to my early childhood, a time of truth and confidence in the fact that there really was a good and gracious force at work in the world, and that it would come to my house.

Actually, there really was a Santa Claus. Oh, it is true that he was greatly changed by many cultures and traditions,

but there was such a man. He was Saint Nicholaus, bishop of Myra, now Demre, in Turkey. He was born around the year 280 in the town of Patara, not far from Myra. Even as a child he was known to be very pious and religious. From the beginning of his life it was said that he wanted to please God, and thus many acts of unusual kindness have been remembered and retold. While these stories are probably immersed in legend, they still give us a good idea of how the original Saint Nicholaus came about.

The most common story told of the saint deals with his saving the virtue of three sisters who were about to be sold into slavery since their poverty-stricken father could not offer the dowry necessary for marriage. The good priest sneaked by the house window one night and threw in three bags of gold. Later legends claimed that he threw the bags down the chimney and they landed in stockings hung by the fire to dry, thus giving us another Christmas tradition. The bags of gold later were symbolized by three balls of gold. The traditional sign that one sees over the door of a pawn-broker—the three gold balls—came about because Nicholaus became the patron saint of pawnbrokers and bankers after he settled with a dishonest borrower.

Greek Orthodox icons of Saint Nicholaus From the author's collection

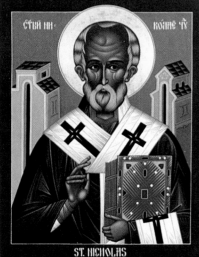

Stories of his calming raging seas, saving seamen, resurrecting crewmen and children, are many. All of the stories, however, point to the kindness of this child of the Church, a kindness that resulted in his giving gifts and offering care, especially to children. When he was declared a saint, he gained a great following simply because he had been kind and approachable during his life. Students, sailors, marriageable young women, even vagabonds and crooks, felt comfortable calling upon him rather than upon the more remote and austere figures within the history of the Church. By the end of the Middle Ages the veneration of Saint Nicholaus had spread from Turkey and Greece into the major portions of the European population.

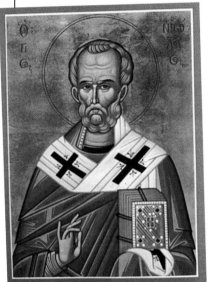

**Byzantine icon
of Saint Nicholaus
From the author's collection**

The peoples of Western Europe, particulary Holland and Germany, saw the Bishop of Myra, Saint Nicholaus, as a bishop of their own time, and dressed him accordingly in their legends. In Dutch his name was pronounced "Sinte Klaas," and the people from Holland who immigrated to this country brought him along with them. In a very short time the name "Sinte Klaas" became Santa Claus . . . but he was still a kind and benevolent bishop.

The Germanic peoples had an image of a "Christkind,"

a young messenger of Christ. With their immigration to the New World came "Christ Kindel," later evolving into Kriss Kringle. They also had a series of pagan elves that lived underground and which would appear driving a sled pulled by two goats named Cracker and Gnasher. All of this sounds quite familiar, doesn't it?

In 1823 Clement Moore, an American minister living in New York, published a wonderful poem entitled "A Visit from Saint Nicholas," in which he translated the image of the saint into that of a little old man, "so lively and quick, I knew in a moment it must be St. Nick." He changed our bishop into this:

> *He was dressed all in fur, from his head to his foot,*
> *And his clothes were all tarnished with ashes and soot;*
> *A bundle of toys he had flung on his back,*
> *And he looked like a pedlar just opening his pack.*
> *His eyes—how they twinkled! his dimples how merry!*
> *His cheeks were like roses, his nose like a cherry!*
> *His droll little mouth was drawn up like a bow,*
> *And the beard of his chin was as white as the snow;*
> *The stump of a pipe he held tight in his teeth,*
> *And the smoke it encircled his head like a wreath;*

**Drawings of Santa Claus by Thomas Nast
from *Harper's Weekly*, c. 1863**

He had a broad face, and a little round belly
That shook, when he laughed, like a bowl full of jelly.
He was chubby and plump, a right jolly old elf,
And I laughed, when I saw him, in spite of myself;
A wink of his eye, and a twist of his head,
Soon gave me to know I had nothing to dread.

This poem was reprinted widely but perhaps never with greater effect than when it appeared in *Harper's Weekly* in 1863 with illustrations by the great Thomas Nast. In Nast's depiction of Santa you can see how closely he resembles the Santa that we know in our time, stripped of his ecclesiastical raiment and returned to his elfish and sometimes pagan origins.

The final influence upon our Santa Claus was to come from the American Corporate Business circle, of course. In

Illustrations of Santa Claus, 1931 (*left*), and 1947 (*right*), commissioned by the Coca-Cola Company. Artist: Haddon Sundblom

1931 the Coca-Cola Company commissioned artist Haddon Sundblom to paint Santa Claus enjoying a bottle of its beverage. Haddon drew upon all of the nineteenth-century illustrators and transformed the popular image of Santa forever. It was Haddon who changed Santa Claus from an often gnomelike figure into the larger-than-life almost godlike image of a serenely smiling all-knowing grandfather.

The Sundblom Santa soon became the accepted portrait of the Christmas saint. For the first time the whole world shared a common idea about Santa's appearance. Sundblom continued to produce a Santa for the Coca-Cola

"Santa Claus," cover illustration from *The Saturday Evening Post,* 1939. Artist: Norman Rockwell

Company annually until his retirement in 1968.

So, we have a short history of a Turkish saint, a bishop at that, who eventually became our Santa Claus. The real question, Virginia, is whether or not he is actually alive today. The images that we have made of him through the centuries obviously have reflected the nature of the times. And, in our time the image of Santa seems to me to be something for which we all hunger. We need a symbol for that caring spirit that every once in a while runs loose in all of us and gives, without excuse or embarrassment, to someone else.

Yes, Santa is alive and well, and I am only fifty-two years old.

Dr. Martin Luther with the legendary Christmas tree

The Christmas Tree

Oh, the stories about the background of the Christmas tree! When I was a child I believed that Christmas trees had always been—just as you did—and I suppose I am a bit disappointed, even at my age, to learn that this was certainly not the case.

There is a very popular legend that claims that Martin Luther conceived of the first Christmas tree one beautiful Christmas Eve. In the beauty of the night and in the stars and the cold he cut a small fir and rushed into the house with it. He placed a few candles on the tree to make present

the stars that he had just seen outside, and the family sat about the tree and sang carols. I like that story and I have a very old etching that shows just such a scene.

However, we must go back further into history. Luther would have done this during the 1500s, but we know that pagan Germanic tribes used the evergreen tree during their worship since the evergreen was an obvious sign of continuing life on earth during a season when most plant life was dying. Such a use of the tree during the winter solstice seems perfectly natural.

The first known written record of the Christmas tree dates from 1603, in Germany. At that time the trees were hung with painted hosts or eucharistic wafers. These were later replaced by ornamental cookies. I still love a tree hung with cookies.

The Germans were very fond of such trees, and when Queen Victoria of England married Prince Albert of Saxe-Coburg-Gotha in 1840, the decorated Christmas tree, which he brought with him to England, swept the British Empire. German immigrants also brought the tree to this country, one story telling of the first Christmas tree coming to America through Hessian mercenaries who fought in the Revolutionary War.

**Jeff's office tree hung with
glass fruits and vegetables**

My wife, Patty, and I celebrated our first Christmas tree as a family during the first December of our marriage. We were in graduate school in theology at Drew University, in Madison, New Jersey. I was serving a parish in Hartsdale/ Scarsdale, New York, at the time, and the head of the county parks division was a member of our parish. Mr. Charles Rapp went out to cut the biggest tree in the park system for a great party in the city square, but when the tree was

felled, the very tip snapped off. No problem, he thought, and he brought the tip of the tree to Patty and me. It was about three feet high. We had little money for decorations, so we made fruit from papier-mâché and hung the tree with the signs of the plenteousness of food and joy in the season. Lord, it was the ugliest tree that I have ever seen, and I think I miss it more than any tree that I have ever known.

Patty with our first Christmas tree in 1964. She is wearing a hero medal because she succeeded in making one papier-maché fruit for the tree. When I asked her what it was she said, "Do you know what a mango looks like?" When I replied, "no," she said, "Then it is a mango!"

_119_

Christmas Carols

Throughout the Middle Ages the word *carol* was associated with dancing songs (derived from the Italian *carolare*, meaning a medieval ring dance accompanied by singing).* By the sixteenth century *carol* had come to mean a song of joy sung at Christmastime in celebration of the Nativity.

The Reformation was not a time for a lot of boisterous singing, so carol singing essentially came to a stop. By the beginning of the nineteenth century carol singing at Christmastime had died out.† Near the end of the nineteenth

*Franklin Watts, ed., *The Complete Christmas Books* (New York: Franklin Watts, 1958), p. 201.
†Miles Hadfield and John Hadfield, *The Twelve Days of Christmas* (Boston: Little, Brown, 1986), p.83.

century, a collection of carols was published, and it was very successful. The publisher included old carols that were discovered in places such as Virginia and Kentucky, where the songs were being sung just as they had hundreds of years earlier. "The Twelve Days of Christmas" was such a carol.

During the last few decades of the 1800s, caroling as a Christmas Feast activity came back into practice and appreciation, both in America and in England. The Puritans in this country, however, were against such joyful outbursts, so it took a while before we really got into the celebration of the carol.

When our boys were little, we used to sing carols during Advent. Our favorite Advent carols were "O Come, O Come, Emmanuel," a ninth-century Latin hymn, and "Come Thou Long-Expected Jesus," by Charles Wesley. The following favorite Christmas carols can be found in any holiday collection of any church hymnal:

"O Little Town of Bethlehem," by
   Phillips Brooks

"Lo, How a Rose E'er Blooming," fifteenth-
   century German

"O Come All Ye Faithful," by
   John Francis Wade

"Hark! The Herald Angels Sing," by
    Charles Wesley

"It Came Upon the Midnight Clear," by
    Edmund H. Sears

"Angels from the Realms of Glory," by
    James Montgomery

"While Shepherds Watched Their Flocks by
    Night," by Nahum Tate

"Angels We Have Heard on High," French
    carol

"Joy to the World," words by Issac Watts,
    music by G. F. Handel

"Away in a Manger"

"God Rest You Merry, Gentlemen," English
    carol

"The First Nowell," English carol

"Silent Night, Holy Night," by Franz Gruber

Gift Giving

Some people in our culture are quite put out that the traditional season of Christmas gift giving has become so terribly commercialized. I can certainly understand their feelings, but gift giving during this holiday goes back to ancient times.

Ancient Germanic and Scandinavian tribes celebrated the festival of Jule at the time of midwinter. The great god Odin was honored at this cold and dark time, and he was a gift giver. He traveled about, bringing the gifts of the coming spring—gifts of grain and new fruit. This mythological figure,

over time, merged with Saint Nicholaus, the historic predecessor of Santa Claus. Further, Saint Nicholaus really did bring gifts to children, and the custom of putting out stockings over the fireplace on Christmas Eve comes directly from the stories about the old saint's kindness.

Finally, the very idea that the Christ Child is God's gift to us should be the chief consideration when thinking about the meaning of gifts during this holy time. The three wise men appear before the Child and bring gifts. And we do the same to those whom we love.

One more ancient legend holds that on Christmas Eve the Christ Child wanders the earth disguised as a beggar, seeking food and shelter. Any mercy shown to the poor and needy becomes a symbolic gesture of love for Jesus. After all, He did say that we are to visit and care for the sick, feed the hungry, and assist those in trouble. "As you did it to one of the least of these my brethen, you did it to me."

Therefore gift giving at Christmas, and the seasonal sense of kindness and good cheer, can really be an act of devotion to the very best things to which we have been called.

I admit that the giving event gets out of hand when it

is aimed only at the showering of countless gifts upon one's own family. Patty and I have always been embarrassed on Christmas morning since we seem to have so much to share with one another, and with our two gorgeous sons. To stop there would be to give in to the commercialization of Christmas. But, as a family, we have always tried to contribute a good deal to the food banks, and we always have a person or two who live alone at our Christmas table. We are not being the good guys. We are simply responding to the call of the tiny Prince of Peace.

Incidentally, did you know that the soup kettles that the wonderful Salvation Army puts out each Christmas for contributions really stem from a true soup kettle? Many years ago in California one of the Salvation Army mission kitchens set out a real soup kettle to collect money for the survivors of a shipwreck. So you see that Christmas need not be handed over to the commercialists. It was given to the meek of heart first, and it can be a holy time for you and your family if you simply keep the true things in perspective.

Christmas Bells

Most of us who live in America have never really heard the sound of many churches pealing their bells all at once. Few churches have such bells in our time, but I remember Sunday mornings in Europe. The din was beautiful, calming, and it made you feel guilty enough to get out of bed and go to church.

Some historians claim that we ring bells on Christmas Eve in order to frighten away the evil spirits of the darkest night of the year, an old pagan custom, of course. And in medieval times the practice developed of having churches

toll, or ring slowly, their bells from eleven o'clock on Christmas Eve to midnight, to warn the evil spirit of the imminent birth of the Child of Bethlehem. This tolling would be followed by the joyous pealing of all of the bells at midnight.

I have no problem with the Church's taking over pagan rites and giving such rites new meaning. But in this case these historians should check their Bibles. In the Book of Exodus, written about three thousand years ago, it is explained that the high priest in the temple was to wear a gown that had a bottom trim of pomegranates—a symbol of seeds and new life—and bells. It is explained quite clearly that the bells will allow those in the Temple to know when the high priest is coming, and when he departs. Our Christmas bells are not necessarily a warning to any dark force . . . but they are a joyous announcement of the fact that the Holy One is coming.

Put bells on your tree, the kind that can really ring. Then, on Christmas Eve, shake the tree and hear the sounds, for the Little King is coming.

CHRISTMAS PUDDINGS AND CAKES

From left to right, clockwise: Figgy Pudding, Hard Sauce, Plum Pudding, Whipped Cream, Whiskey Sauce, Steamed Date Pudding (Toby mugs pictured traditionally hold sauces for puddings in England)

Figgy Pudding

SERVES 12

½   cup (1 stick) butter, at room temperature

2   eggs

1   cup molasses

2   cups dried figs (about 1 pound), stems removed, chopped fine

½   teaspoon grated lemon peel

1   cup buttermilk

½   cup walnuts, chopped

2½   cups all-purpose flour

½   teaspoon baking soda

2   teaspoons baking powder

1   teaspoon salt

½   teaspoon ground cinnamon

¼   teaspoon ground nutmeg

Garnish
> Whipped cream or Hard Sauce (page 140)

Our love of puddings and heavy cakes most often come from the influence of the English. How they ate . . . and they brought this love of sweets to the New World from the very beginning.

"Now brings us a figgy pudding. . . ." And that is what we are going to do!

In an electric mixer, cream the butter until fluffy. Add the eggs and molasses and beat again. Add the figs, lemon peel, buttermilk, and walnuts and blend 1 minute. Add the remaining ingredients and blend until everything is incorporated. Grease and flour an 8 × 4-inch soufflé dish and pour in the batter. Bake in a 325° oven for 1 hour, or until a toothpick inserted in the center comes out clean. Spoon the pudding out onto plates or cut it into wedges. Garnish with the whipped cream.

Plum Pudding

SERVES 8

½   cup (1 stick) butter, at room temperature

1   cup sugar

6   eggs, at room temperature

½   cup chopped citron

1 ½   cups pitted prunes, chopped

½   cup dark raisins

1   cup pecans, coarsely chopped

½   cup all-purpose flour

1 ½   cups fine bread crumbs

1   teaspoon ground cinnamon

1   teaspoon ground nutmeg

½   teaspoon ground allspice

Garnish
Whipped cream or Hard Sauce (page 140)

Cream the butter and sugar together in an electric mixer. Beat the eggs in, one at a time. Combine the citron, prunes, raisins, and pecans in another bowl. Add the flour to the fruit and nuts and toss together so that everything is coated with flour. Add to the butter and egg mixture along with the remaining ingredients. Blend for 1 minute so that all is incorporated. Grease and flour a soufflé dish, about 7 × 4 inches. Add the heavy batter and bake in a preheated 350° oven for 50 to 55 minutes, or until nicely browned. Serve warm by spooning out or cool and cut into pieces. Garnish with the whipped cream or hard sauce.

We are going to use pitted prunes, or dried plums, in this old English classic. This is so rich and so wonderful that upon eating you will feel as wealthy as one of the Wise Men.

Steamed Date Pudding with Whiskey Sauce

SERVES 8

The romance behind Charles Dickens's Christmas Carol is to be found in this pudding. It is boiled in water and served steaming hot. Surely, this would help your family feel more Christmas-y.

- ½ cup (1 stick) butter, at room temperature
- 1 cup honey
- 1 tablespoon grated lemon peel
- 1 teaspoon lemon juice
- 2 eggs
- ¾ cup chopped pitted dates
- ½ cup chopped pecans
- 2 cups all-purpose flour
- 1 ½ teaspoons baking powder
- ½ teaspoon salt
- ½ teaspoon ground cinnamon
- ½ teaspoon ground nutmeg
- ½ teaspoon ground cloves
- 1 cup milk

With an electric mixer, beat the butter and honey together until smooth. Add the lemon peel and lemon juice and blend again. Beat in the eggs, one at a time. Mix the dates and pecans with 2 tablespoons of the flour and set aside.

Sift together the remaining flour with the other dry ingredients. Add the dry ingredients to the creamed mixture alternately with the milk. Stir in the dates and nuts.

Butter a 2-quart mold, including the lid. If the mold has no lid, butter some aluminum foil and tie it on the mold as a lid. Pour the batter into the mold and cover. (You could also use a 2-pound coffee can as a mold.) Place the mold in a large pot and add water to come halfway up the sides of

the mold. Bring the water to a boil, cover the pot, and simmer for 2 hours, or until the pudding pulls away from the sides of the mold. Let stand 10 minutes before unmolding. This may be done before dessert time. If necessary, simply reheat in a standard oven at about 325°. Serve with Whiskey Sauce.

The Whiskey Sauce
½ cup (1 stick) butter

1 cup confectioners' sugar

1 egg, well beaten

2 tablespoons whiskey, or more to taste

In a double boiler, cook the butter and sugar until the sugar is completely dissolved and very hot. Remove from the heat. Add the beaten egg, using a whisk, so that it will not curdle. When very smooth, allow to cool. Add the whiskey to taste.

Hard Sauce

MAKES ABOUT ½ CUP

½ cup (1 stick) unsalted butter (softened)

½ cup confectioners' sugar

3 tablespoons rum or brandy

Cream the butter and confectioners' sugar together until fluffy. Beat in the rum or brandy, 1 tablespoon at a time. Place in a serving bowl. Chill until firm, but let come to room temperature when ready to serve.

Christmas Fruitcakes

When I was a boy, my mother made fruitcake every year. It was as heavy as lead, and we ate it just about as slowly. Calvin Trillin, the great and humorous food writer, claims that there is only one fruitcake in existence, and it just keeps getting passed around every Christmas.

This one you can eat, but remember to make it some weeks ahead of time. I cannot remember the source of this dish, but I owe someone some thanks, so if this is your recipe, published in some newspaper somewhere some years ago, call me, and we will have dinner. This is first class!

Bourbon Fruitcake

SERVES THE NEIGHBORHOOD

2   cups mixed candied fruit, chopped coarse
1   cup candied cherries, halved
3   cups raisins
1   cup currants
½   cup bourbon
1   cup (2 sticks) butter, at room temperature
1   cup firmly packed brown sugar
6   eggs, at room temperature
½   ounce unsweetened chocolate, melted
3   cups walnuts, coarsely chopped
2   cups all-purpose flour
1   teaspoon ground nutmeg
1   teaspoon ground cloves
½   teaspoon baking soda
¾   teaspoon salt
½   cup brandy

In a large bowl, combine the candied fruits, raisins, currants, and bourbon. Mix well, cover, and marinate 3 hours on the counter.

Cream together the butter and brown sugar until fluffy (I use my KitchenAid mixer). Beat in the eggs, one at a time. Add the melted chocolate, walnuts, and the marinated fruit along with the bourbon. Blend for a minute and add the flour, nutmeg, cloves, baking soda, and salt. Mix well until all is incorporated. Pack the heavy batter into a greased 10 × 4-inch tube pan. Bake in a preheated 300° oven for 2 hours and 10 minutes. Remove to a rack. When the cake

is cool enough to handle, remove it from the pan and cool on the rack.

Place the cooled cake in a stainless-steel pot with a lid and drizzle half the brandy over it. Cover and allow to rest on the counter for 1 week. After 1 week, drizzle with the remaining brandy, cover, and allow to rest another week. Slice and serve. This cake will keep for months in the refrigerator.

Gram's Lighter Applesauce Fruitcake

MAKES 3 2-POUND LOAVES

1 cup (2 sticks) butter, at room temperature

2 cups sugar

2 eggs, at room temperature

2 teaspoons vanilla

2 cups pitted dates, chopped coarse

3 cups applesauce

2 cups walnuts, chopped coarse

2 cups raisins

2 cups mixed candied fruit, chopped coarse

½ teaspoon salt

1 teaspoon ground cinnamon

½ teaspoon ground cloves

1 tablespoon baking soda

4 cups all-purpose flour

Cream the butter and sugar together (I use my KitchenAid mixer). Beat in the eggs, one at a time, along with the vanilla. Add the remaining ingredients and blend until all is incorporated. Divide the batter among 3 greased loaf pans, approximately 8 × 4 × 3 inches each. Bake in a preheated 350° oven for 1 hour and 15 minutes, or until a toothpick inserted in the center comes out clean. Remove to a cooling rack. When cool enough to handle, remove the loaves from the pans and cool completely on the rack. Wrap in plastic wrap and keep in the refrigerator.

As my mother grew older, her tastes changed. All of us pass through such a thing. Finally, by the grace of God, she stopped making those heavy, dark fruitcakes. This new version is of her new mind, and I like it very much. It is simple to prepare. Incidentally, all of her grandchildren have always called my mother "Gram."

From left to right: **Lemon Cream Cookies, Gingerbread Cookies, Peppermint Candy Cookies, Cookie Ornaments for the Tree (hanging), Rosettes, Oatmeal Crispies, Babes Wrapped in Swaddling Clothes**

Christmas
Cookies

Gingerbread Cookies

MAKES ABOUT 8 LARGE
GINGERBREAD PEOPLE

Gingerbread cookies are really an old English custom. I do not necessarily like to eat them, but I sure like to make them. Buy a large (about 8 inches) cookie cutter from your local gourmet shop and have a field day! You can decorate them with a simple piping bag and a basic confectioners' sugar icing. Such fun!

¾ cup (1½ sticks) butter, at room temperature
¾ cup firmly packed dark brown sugar
½ cup dark molasses
1 tablespoon fresh lemon juice
4½ cups all-purpose flour
1½ teaspoons baking soda
½ teaspoon ground cloves
1 teaspoon ground cinnamon
2½ teaspoons ground ginger
¼ teaspoon ground cardamom
½ teaspoon ground nutmeg
1 teaspoon salt
3 tablespoons cold water

Cream the butter and brown sugar together until fluffy (I use my KitchenAid mixer). Add the molasses and lemon juice and beat again. Combine all the dry ingredients in a separate bowl. Add the dry ingredients to the butter mixture and blend until crumbly. Add the cold water and mix until a dough is formed. Knead a minute by hand so that the dough holds together. Wrap the dough in plastic wrap and refrigerate 1½ hours.

Roll the dough out to a ¼-inch thickness on a lightly floured surface. Cut the figures out of the dough with a gingerbread man or woman cookie cutter. Arrange the figures on a nonstick cookie sheet. Bake in a preheated 350° oven for 15 to 20 minutes, or until the edges of the cookies begin to turn brown.

Babes Wrapped in Swaddling Clothes

MAKES 4 ½ DOZEN

Dawn Sparks, our secretary and a woman of extreme charm and joy, offered this recipe from her childhood. It is a tasty and fun cookie to make for your children.

The Dough

- **4 cups all-purpose flour**
- **1 teaspoon salt**
- **1 cup (2 sticks) butter**
- **1 8-ounce container sour cream**
- **2 egg yolks (reserve the whites for the meringue filling below)**
- **1 tablespoon lemon juice**
   Confectioners' sugar

Combine the flour and salt in a mixing bowl. Cut in the butter until grainy. In a small bowl, combine the sour cream, egg yolks, and lemon juice. Blend the sour cream mixture into the flour mixture. Knead together to form a smooth dough. Place the dough on plastic wrap and pat it into a 6 × 8-inch rectangle. Wrap and refrigerate 2 hours, or overnight.

The Filling

- **2 egg whites, reserved from making the dough**
- **½ cup sugar**
- **1 cup walnuts, chopped fine**
- **2 ½ teaspoons ground cinnamon**
- **¼ teaspoon salt**

Whip the egg whites until stiff but not dry. Gradually whip in the sugar to form a meringue. Whip until the meringue holds soft peaks. Fold in the remaining ingredients.

Dust a rolling pin and the counter with flour. Roll the chilled dough out into a thin (⅛ inch maximum) rectangle on the floured counter. Trim the edges so the rectangle measures 24 × 15 inches. Cut the dough into 3-inch squares and dust with confectioners' sugar. Place a rounded teaspoon of the filling in the center of each dough square. With a tiny bit of water, dampen two opposite corners. Fold the two opposite corners over each other and press the center together lightly. Place the cookies on a nonstick baking sheet and bake in a preheated 350° oven for 30 minutes, or until lightly browned.

Sesame Cookies

MAKES ABOUT 3 DOZEN

¾ cup (1 ½ sticks) butter, at room temperature

½ cup confectioners' sugar

1 teaspoon vanilla

4 tablespoons sesame oil

2½ cups all-purpose flour

2 tablespoons cold water, or more to form a dough

¾ cup raw sesame seeds

Cream the butter and the sugar with the vanilla and sesame oil (I use my KitchenAid mixer). Blend in the flour until incorporated. Add the 2 tablespoons cold water, or more, to form a dough. Roll the dough into 1-inch balls, then roll the balls in the sesame seeds. Place on a baking sheet 2 inches apart from each other. Bake in a preheated 350° for about 25 to 30 minutes, or until the sesame seeds begin to turn golden brown and the insides of the cookies are not doughy.

We added this cookie recipe to the bunch since we thought that you should taste a flavor very common to the time of the Child. Sesame seeds were used in everyday cooking, as was sesame oil, so we have put them upon a butter cookie. The result is very delicious.

Lemon Cream Cookies

MAKES 6 DOZEN

The Dough

¾ cup (1 ½ sticks) butter, at room temperature

3 ounces cream cheese, softened

1 tablespoon baking powder

½ teaspoon salt

1 cup sugar

1 egg, at room temperature

1 tablespoon grated lemon peel

1 tablespoon fresh lemon juice

3 cups all-purpose flour, or more

My mother has been making these cookies for as long as I can remember. I really doubt that Christmas morning would ever arrive if she were not to make these for the new dawn.

Cream the butter and cream cheese together until fluffy (I use my KitchenAid mixer). Blend in the baking powder, salt, sugar, egg, grated lemon peel, and the lemon juice. Gradually blend in the 3 cups flour, or more, and knead to form a soft dough. Force the dough through a cookie press (Sawa brand from Sweden) with a number 16 plate to form 3-inch-long cookie bars (see photo). Press the cookies directly onto a baking sheet. Bake in a preheated 400° oven for 8 to 10 minutes. Allow to cool on a rack.

The Icing

1 cup confectioners' sugar

½ teaspoon fresh lemon juice

4 teaspoons milk

⅔ cup walnuts, chopped fine

In a small bowl, blend the sugar, lemon juice, and milk together until smooth. Brush half the top of the cookie with icing. Sprinkle the icing with the nuts. Place the cookie on a rack to dry the icing. Repeat the process.

Photograph courtesy of Williams-Sonoma

Oatmeal Crispies

MAKES ABOUT 8 DOZEN

1 ½   cups all-purpose flour

  1   teaspoon salt

  3   cups Quaker Oats Quick Oats

 ½   cup walnuts, chopped fine

  1   teaspoon vanilla

  1   cup shortening

  2   cups firmly packed light brown sugar

  2   eggs, beaten

  1   teaspoon baking soda

  1   teaspoon grated orange peel

  1   teaspoon ground cinnamon

  1   teaspoon ground nutmeg

In a a bowl, combine all the ingredients and knead together to form a dough. Place half the dough, shaped into a rough rope, on a large piece of plastic wrap. Fold the plastic over and work the dough into the shape of a log 2 inches in diameter. Repeat with the remaining dough. Freeze the logs until hard, about 2 hours.

To make the cookies, cut the dough into ³⁄₁₆-inch slices and place on nonstick cookie sheets. Bake in a preheated 350° oven for 10 to 12 minutes. Transfer to a rack to cool or eat them warm from the oven.

This is another cookie that my mother has made for me since . . . well, I simply cannot remember. They are simple to make and pure in flavor. This is real Grandma-type stuff!

Rosettes

Mom made these years ago and then told me that she could not remember the recipe. I did remember that she put cardamom in hers as she is very Norwegian. So, I saw this recipe in one of the best basic cookbooks of our time, The Joy of Cooking, and I added the cardamom. These are fun to make!

2   eggs, beaten
¼   teaspoon salt
½   teaspoon ground cardamom
1   tablespoon sugar
1   cup all-purpose flour
1   cup milk
2   tablespoons butter, melted
    Peanut oil for frying

Garnish
    Confectioners' sugar

Beat the eggs, salt, cardamom, and sugar together in a mixing bowl. Beat the flour and milk alternately into the mixture. Stir in the melted butter.

To make rosettes, heat the peanut oil to 375° (1½ inches of oil in an electric frying pan works great for this). Dip a rosette iron into the hot oil, then into the batter. Do not let the batter run over the top of the iron as this may make it difficult for the rosette to release. Immerse the batter-coated iron in the hot oil until the rosette comes free. Fry for 20 to 25 seconds. Remove the rosette to drain on paper towels. Reheat the iron in the oil and repeat the process. Dust with the confectioners' sugar.

Cookie Ornaments for the Tree

MAKES ONE DOZEN ORNAMENTS

1 ³/₄ cups hot water

1 cup salt

4 cups all-purpose flour

Egg Wash
1 egg, beaten with 3 tablespoons water

Pour the hot water into a bowl with the salt and stir for 1 minute (I use my KitchenAid mixer). The salt grains will reduce in size, but they will not completely dissolve. Add the flour and blend until all the water is absorbed. Turn the dough onto a floured surface and knead a few minutes until it is smooth and pliable. Cover the dough and allow to rest for 5 minutes. Keep the dough in a plastic bag if you do not plan to use it after the 5 minutes of resting time.

Roll the dough out ³/₈ inch thick on a floured surface and cut out shapes with cookie cutters. Place the cookies on a nonstick baking sheet and brush lightly with the egg wash. Bake in a preheated 300° oven for 1 hour and 15 minutes, or until golden brown. You can also press the dough into lightly oiled fancy ceramic molds* or lightly floured wooden molds and bake as instructed by the manufacturer.

*Decorative ceramic cookie molds can be obtained from Brown Bag Cookie Art by Hill Design, Inc., 7 Eagle Square, Concord, New Hampshire 03301.

No, Virginia, you cannot eat these cookies. The dough is made of salt and flour and it will last several years. Our secretary, Dawn Sparks, gave us this recipe from her daughter-in-law, Becky. It works very well. A tree decorated with cookies is one of the most delightful things a child could ever see, even though he cannot eat the cookies. Nevertheless, he understands that Christmastime is to be a time of endless enjoyment.

Peppermint Candy Cookies

MAKES 3 DOZEN

This is another of my mother's treasures. She wastes nothing—that is how I learned to be frugal—and I have seen her save the leftover candy canes from the year before and use them to make this charming cookie.

The Dough

1   cup (2 sticks) butter, softened (do not substitute margarine or shortening)

½   cup confectioners' sugar

1   teaspoon vanilla

2½   cups all-purpose flour

½   cup walnuts, chopped

Cream the butter, sugar, and vanilla together until fluffy. Add the flour and walnuts and blend to form a dough. Wrap in plastic wrap and chill for 1 hour.

Candy Mixture for Garnish

¼   pound peppermint candy, crushed fine

½   cup confectioners' sugar

In a small bowl, combine both ingredients. Set aside. Three tablespoons of this mixture is used in the filling below and the remainder is used to garnish the cookies.

The Filling

2   tablespoons cream cheese, softened

1   teaspoon milk

1   drop red food coloring

½   cup confectioners' sugar

3   tablespoons candy mixture (see above)

In a bowl, blend together the cream cheese, milk, food coloring, and the confectioner's sugar until smooth. Blend in the 3 tablespoons candy mixture.

Remove the dough from the refrigerator and for each cookie pinch off a rounded teaspoon of the dough. Form into a ball and shape the dough around your thumb to make a little compartment in the middle. Place about $1/4$ teaspoon of the cream cheese filling in the depression. Pinch the dough back together and roll it back into a ball. Repeat the process with the remaining dough and filling. Place the balls on a nonstick cookie sheet. Bake in a preheated 350° oven for 10 to 12 minutes. Do not brown.

Remove the cookies to a cooling rack. To garnish, roll the cooled cookies in the remaining candy mixture.

Mincemeat Pie

This dish came from England, of course. But please remember that the ingredients represent a joining together of a major portion of the Western world, not just England. It was the Romans that brought their love of dried fruits with them to England, and they had learned to make same from the Greeks! So, we have several cultures here and thus a great way to celebrate the birth of the One who is called The King of Kings.

Mincemeat

This is my mother's recipe. It actually contains meat and it is just delicious. Jason, my son, is very interested in Christmas dinner, but more interested in Gram's mincemeat. If my mother were to make this in March, I really think Jason would fly home to Washington from college in New Jersey.

2 ½   pounds beef stew meat

5   pounds Granny Smith apples, cored and chopped but not peeled

¾   pound beef suet, coarsely ground

1 ½   pounds dark raisins

½   pound mixed candied peel, chopped

1   pound brown sugar

1   cup distilled white vinegar

½   cup molasses

1   pound currants

1   cup apple juice

1 ½   teaspoons ground cloves

1 ½   teaspoons ground nutmeg

1 ½   teaspoons ground allspice

1 ½   teaspoons ground cinnamon

Place the stew meat in a 4-quart pot and add just enough water to cover. Bring to a boil, cover, and simmer 1 hour. Drain the meat and grind coarse.

Place the ground meat in an 8-quart pot along with the remaining ingredients. Stir together and bring to a simmer. Cover and simmer gently for 1 hour, stirring the mixture occasionally. Allow to cool. The filling is ready to use, or pack it into 1-quart canning jars and freeze for later use. It makes a great Christmas gift.

Mincemeat Pie

MAKES 1 PIE

1 quart Mincemeat (page 166)
1 Granny Smith apple, cored and chopped but not peeled
1 recipe Basic Easy Crust (below)

Egg Wash
1 egg, beaten with 2 tablespoons water

Combine the mincemeat pie filling with the apple and place in the bottom of pie crust. Spread out evenly.

Cut ½-inch strips out of the remaining dough and lay over the filling in a lattice design. Brush lattice strips with the egg wash. Bake in a preheated 375° oven for 1 hour, until golden brown and bubbly.

Basic Easy Crust

MAKES A 9-INCH TOP AND
BOTTOM CRUST

3 cups all-purpose flour
1 teaspoon salt
½ cup (1 stick) margarine
½ cup Crisco
1 egg
1 tablespoon white vinegar
3 to 4 tablespoons ice water

In a medium bowl, stir together the flour and salt. Using a pastry blender, cut in the margarine and shortening. Keep

Please do not even talk to me about a mincemeat pie from a bakery or a supermarket freezer. This is the real stuff, and when you serve it, even after all this work, raise your head high!

working the flour and shortening until the mixture is rather grainy, like coarse cornmeal. Mix the egg and vinegar together and, using a wooden fork, stir the mixture into the flour. Add enough of the ice water so that the dough barely holds together. Place on a marble pastry board or a plastic countertop and knead for just a few turns, enough so that the dough holds together and becomes rollable. I roll out my dough on a piece of waxed paper. It is easy to handle that way. If you have a marble rolling pin, the rolling out will be easy. If you use a wooden one, be sure to dust a teaspoon of flour on it a couple of times when you are rolling out the dough.

169

The Festival
of Lights
and Chanukah

Lights and candles have always played an important role during this darkest night of the year, the winter solstice. The custom goes back to ancient Greece and Rome.

In the Christian tradition Jesus is called "The Light of the World," and thus our Christmas trees are adorned with lights and the windows filled with candles and tapers. Even the flaming plum pudding plays with the tradition of light on the eve of the Christ.

One of the favorite customs of the season that has always been enjoyed in our home is that of the Jewish Fes-

tival of the Lights, called Chanukah. The holiday lasts for eight evenings and on each night a new candle is lighted on the Chanukah menorah, the holiday candle holder. Finally, at the end of the period, all nine candles are ablaze and the home feels wonderfully warm and filled with light. And, on each of the eight nights, children are given a small present, a custom that my two sons, Channing and Jason, always thought to be profound and sensible.

Since this splendid winter holiday comes from a Biblical story, it can be celebrated by all of us who trace our theological lineage back to Abraham, Isaac, and Jacob. The story is fascinating and typical not only of the pains heaped upon the Jews for centuries, but it is also typical of their faith and perseverance.

> *The story goes back to about 165 B.C. At that time*
> *all that remained of the Kingdom of Judah was*
> *under the rule of Antiochus Epiphanes, King of*
> *Syria, who demanded that all his subjects worship*
> *the Greek gods and adopt the Greek way of life.*
> *This the Jews refused to do. Judas Maccabeus, a*
> *devout Jewish leader, with the help of his four*
> *brothers, led the Jews in a victorious struggle*

against their Syrian oppressors. Their victory made it possible for the Jews to worship once again in their Temple in Jerusalem, and it eventually led to the re-establishment of the Kingdom of Judah. It was, in fact, the first great victory for religious freedom in the world.

When Jerusalem was again theirs, the first concern of the Jews was to cleanse their beloved Temple of all traces of idolatrous worship. The great Menorah (candelabrum) was returned to its place in the court. When the people turned to relight the Perpetual Light, they found that all but one cruet of holy oil had been defiled. This was only enough oil for one day, but when it was lighted, a miracle occurred: the oil burned for the full eight days required to replenish the supply.*

Judas Maccabeus proclaimed an eight-day festival to keep us mindful of the miracle of the lights, and he called the event Chanukah, which means "dedication." It was not the battle that was so important, but rather the rededication

*From Fannie Engle and Gertrude Blair, *The Jewish Festival Cookbook* (New York: David McKay Company, 1954), pp. 79–80.

of the temple and the realization that the Holy One always anticipates our needs . . . and fulfills them. Our rabbi in Tacoma, Richard Rosenthal, puts it this way: "The joy of Chanukah comes not from the defeat of the enemy but from the rededication of the temple. It is significant that the prophetic reading on the Sabbath of Chanukah has, as its keynote, 'Not by might, nor by power, but by My Spirit, says the Lord of hosts (Zechariah 4:6)."

You can find a copy of the home service for Chanukah at any temple or synagogue. As is typical of Jewish worship, this holiday is celebrated in the home rather than in a formal institution. You can have great fun lighting each of the candles as the holiday goes on. My sons always love to hear a story after dinner, a story by the renowned Jewish storyteller Isaac Bashevis Singer. We have a copy of *When Shlemiel Went to Warsaw & Other Stories*. It is hilarious and brilliant and touching and profound . . . as is Chanukah. We always played with the dreidel, a little top that is spun by each family member, and you literally gamble for chocolate coins covered with gold foil, *geld*.

Now that the boys are off to college, we don't celebrate this very family holiday any more. We should, and I think you should too.

One of our favorite meals for the Chanukah is latkes, crisp potato pancakes, and tzimmes, a beef brisket baked with sweet potatoes, onions, and prunes. This is a great menu, but you should probably throw in a salad or two. Then light the candles, tell the darkness of December to stand back, and give thanks for our forefathers and foremothers in the faith.

CHANUKAH DINNER

Latkes

Tzimmes

Latkes

This dish simply is basic to Chanukah. Jack Markovitz, a student of mine when I was a college chaplain, made this for our family one night, and we keep making them every year. Jack, where are you? I would love a call.

2 cups coarsely grated potatoes, peeled
1 egg, beaten
1 teaspoon salt
½ medium yellow onion, peeled and chopped fine
  Peanut oil for frying
½ pint sour cream
1 cup applesauce

Squeeze as much water as possible out of the potatoes. In a bowl, mix with the remaining ingredients. Place a bit of the mixture spread out to 4 inches in a frying pan containing a little peanut oil. Fry until golden brown on both sides. Serve the pancakes with a bit of sour cream and applesauce on top of each.

Tzimmes

SERVES 6 TO 8

1 4-pound beef brisket
   Salt and freshly ground black pepper to taste
2 medium yellow onions, peeled and chopped coarse
2 ribs celery, chopped coarse
¼ cup chopped fresh parsley
3 cups Beef Stock (page 274)
   Juice of 1 lemon
3 whole cloves
1 ½-inch piece cinnamon stick or ½ teaspoon ground cinnamon
2½ pounds sweet potatoes, peeled and quartered
5 medium carrots, peeled and cut into 2-inch pieces
1 12-ounce box pitted prunes
1 tablespoon honey
2 tablespoons distilled white vinegar

Season the brisket lightly with salt and pepper. Place the meat on a rack in a large roasting pan. Brown the beef, fatty side up, in a preheated 475° oven for 25 minutes. Remove the meat on the rack and set aside. Add the onions, celery, and parsley to the roasting pan. Place the browned brisket on top of the vegetables, without the roasting rack. Add the beef stock, lemon juice, cloves, and cinnamon stick. Cover the pan with a lid or aluminum foil. Reduce the oven temperature to 300° and bake the brisket for 2 hours and 15 minutes. Remove the pan from the oven and add the sweet potatoes, carrots, and the prunes. Mix the honey with the vinegar and pour over the meat. Return the pan to the oven and bake, covered, for 1 hour and 15 minutes more. Season with salt and pepper to taste. Slice the meat and serve with the vegetables and sauce that has formed in the pan.

There are as many variations on this dish as there are Jewish grandmas. Really! I originally found this recipe in a wonderful magazine common on the West Coast called Sunset. I think that this journal offers some of the best recipes in the country.

Christmas 1976 Jason and Channing front, Jeff and Patty back

Christmas 1973 Jason, Patty, Channing, and Jeff

Snapshots of Patty, Jeff, Channing, and Jason from family Christmases in times past

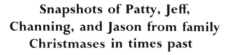

Christmas 1973 Channing (foreground) and Jason

Our Family Christmas

Our family traditions came about in much the same way as did your family traditions . . . they just sort of happened.

Patty and I originally made a roast prime rib of beef for Christmas, and then the boys came along. Somehow Patty got into the roast goose routine, and we enjoyed that for years. As the boys grew, we began to celebrate one of the Christmas menus that follow, and then on Christmas Day I would prepare a full Norwegian smorgasbord with baked beans, potato salad, several different kinds of her-

ring, luncheon meats, special breads, fish balls in cream sauce, cold salmon or lox, *lefse,* Christmas bread, and, of course, the leftover roast beef or goose from the night before. We still do that.

Last year I did a Swedish meal of pickled pork. The Paulina Market in Chicago makes a Swedish pickled fresh ham that is just terrific. So, now we all have a new favorite dinner. The boys side with the goose, Patty with the roast beef, and I go for the pickled ham. Now what do we do?

One year I suggested to Jason that we make some changes in our Christmas dinners. Try something new. He was quite young at the time, but his response meant that we had established some family traditions that he wanted to maintain. I was so touched by his insight that I wrote the following letter to him, a letter that was circulated by a Roman Catholic parish in Chicago. You will probably recognize your own family in this letter.

A Letter to Jason

My dear Jason,

I probably came very close to violating the meaning of tradition when I suggested that we try something a bit different this year. You are happily bound up in memories of Christmases past, and I expect that I will hear you say, "Dad, can't we have real dressing? I mean the old kind. After all, it is Christmas!"

You are right, son, it is Christmas. And on the day of the Mass, the feast of Christ, I should not go around breaking family traditions.

But I must consider anew the meaning of the Feast of the Christmas, and I think you and I should think about it together.

The term feast *is very much involved with the meaning of memory. We feast because we remember certain events in our lives; sometimes wonderful events, sometimes painful events. That seems to be the way it has been with man- and womankind for a long time.*

Christmas for me as a child was very different from our Christmas now. We would travel to greet my father's family at his mother's house, your great-grandmother, Nettie Smith. Oh how sad I feel that you did not know this tough old girl. She was a member of the state legislature and she was a left-winger from the start. But in the kitchen she was just terrible. She cooked turkey in the Old Testament style, burning the poor thing on the altar until smoke drifted up to heaven. Then, to the table it would come, though it was so desiccated, so dried out, so tasteless, that I could not understand why someone else in the family did not cook the bird instead. You know why they did not? Because it was a job traditionally reserved for Gramma. To this day, when I eat dried-out turkey, I think of her . . . and how much I miss her.

Christmas morning in my family was wonderful. World War II was in the midst of every event, and candy and sugar were hard to find. One Yule morning my mother, your Grandma Smith, brought us to the table and presented us with

marzipan candy shaped like eggs and bacon. My brother, Greg, sister, Judy, and I were amazed that Mom could find such things.

Some of our Christmas traditions are a bit strange, I will admit. But they are our traditions, our family. Each year we carefully unpack the papier-mâché manger figures we made together when you and Channing were tiny children. And each year we spend precious time gluing the poor shepherd boy back together. Would it not be much more practical simply to go out and buy a new crèche, a new king, a new Christ Child? Ah, now, my boy, we are speaking of utter heresy, of violations against the meaning of our past . . . and I suppose therefore, our future.

A true feast actually has nothing to do with what you eat . . . but with what you remember. Many families in this nation have no traditions at all, few roots, and, thus, few feasts. I am for feasting and celebrating in such a way that we will always remember we are a family. Sometimes I know that it is tough having me for a father, since

I always want to add sherry to a gravy that you find perfectly in order already. Or I want to put mushrooms in a dressing, and you claim that they taste like dirt.

So, now, back to the kitchen. We have much to prepare before the star grows bright over the manger and you and I come to the crèche, dazed by what we find, but carrying two gravies. One with mushrooms and one without.

> *I love you,*
> *Dad*

FAVORITE CHRISTMAS MENUS

CHRISTMAS
ROAST BEEF DINNER

Roast Prime Rib of Beef

Yorkshire Pudding

Creamed Onions

Wine Sauce for Beef

Horseradish Sauce

**Gravy for
Yorkshire Pudding**

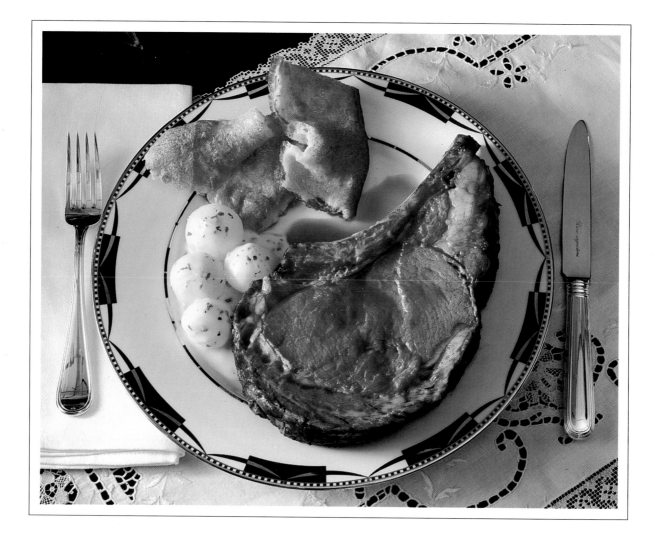

Roast Prime Rib of Beef

SERVES 10 TO 12

Freshly ground black pepper to taste

1 **tablespoon dark soy sauce**

1 ½ **tablespoons Kitchen Bouquet**

1 **tablespoon dry Colman's mustard**

1 **8- to 9-pound beef rib roast, bone in**

1 **cup peeled and sliced (⅛ inch thick) yellow onion**

Rub the seasonings on the roast in the order listed. Pack the sliced onion on the roast. Place the roast on a rack in a roasting pan. Roast in a preheated 450° oven 20 minutes. Reduce the oven temperature to 325° and roast 1 hour more. Reduce the oven again to 300° and roast about 1 hour more, or until the beef registers 115° for rare in the center when tested with a meat thermometer. Remove from the oven and allow to stand 15 minutes in a warm place. Slice and serve immediately with Wine Sauce for Beef (page 200).

Asking me to name my favorite Christmas meal is like asking me to tell you which son I love more. It is an impossible task! However, this one is terrific. The recipe for the beef comes from my beloved friend Dr. Lester Baskin. It is simple to prepare, but you must not overcook it. You will enjoy the rest of the menu, a menu that was common in our house for many years. I still love it.

Yorkshire Pudding

⬡

This recipe is from **The Joy of Cooking,** *one of the finest and most basic cookbooks ever to come on the market. It is easy to prepare, but you should use a heavy frying pan, one that will hold some heat.*

⅞ **(1 scant) cup all-purpose flour**

½ **teaspoon salt**

½ **cup milk, at room temperature**

2 **eggs, beaten, at room temperature**

½ **cup water, at room temperature**

2 **tablespoons fat drippings from the roasting pan or 2 tablespoons olive oil**

Blend the flour and salt together in a mixing bowl. Form a well in the center of the flour. Stir the milk in and beat until light and airy. Stir in the eggs and the water and beat the batter until large bubbles rise to the surface. Heat a 10-inch ovenproof SilverStone frying pan until very hot. Add the fat drippings and quickly pour the batter into the hot frying pan. Cook over high heat for a few seconds. Place the pan in a preheated 400° oven and bake for 20 minutes. Reduce the oven temperature to 350° and continue baking 5 to 10 minutes more, until puffy and golden brown. Remove to a serving plate or serve right out of the frying pan, being careful not to burn anyone.

Creamed Onions

SERVES 6

3   pounds small yellow onions (larger than pearl onions)

2   cups Chicken Stock (page 275)

3   tablespoons butter

6   tablespoons all-purpose flour

1   cup half-and-half

¼   cup dry sherry
     Salt and freshly ground white pepper to taste

⅛   teaspoon ground nutmeg

2   tablespoons chopped fresh parsley

Trim the ends of the onions and peel. Place the onions in a saucepan and add the chicken stock. Bring to a boil, cover, and simmer 10 minutes, or until just tender. Strain, reserving the stock, and set the onions aside. Return the stock to the pan and bring to a simmer.

In a small frying pan, melt the butter and add the flour. Cook together to make a roux. Do not brown. Add the roux to the hot stock and whisk until smooth and thickened. Stir in the half-and-half and sherry and simmer 2 minutes more. Add salt and white pepper to taste, the nutmeg, and parsley. Combine the cream sauce with the onions and place in a small round ovenproof casserole. Bake in a preheated 375° oven for 35 to 45 minutes until hot and bubbly. Brown the top under the broiler, if you wish.

All right, so I am the only one who eats these on Christmas Eve. I love them and I keep thinking that someday my wife and my boys will grow up to the point where they love the onions as well. So far, no luck. I hope, however, that you love them.

Wine Sauce for Beef

MAKES ABOUT 2 CUPS

2 ½   cups Beef Stock (page 274)
 ½   cup dry red wine
      Salt to taste

Bring the beef stock and wine to a boil in a small saucepan. Simmer, uncovered, until reduced to 2 cups. Add any pan drippings from the rib roast to the sauce. Strain the sauce and skim off as much fat as possible. Add salt to taste. Serve with roasted beef.

Horseradish Sauce

MAKES ³/₄ CUP

¼   cup prepared horseradish
¼   cup sour cream
¼   cup mayonnaise

In a bowl, combine all the ingredients. Serve with beef.

I prefer a light wine sauce for good beef, but gravy for the Yorkshire pudding. Thus this recipe.

Do you want to talk about simple? This is it, and I see no room for improvement. With a little wine sauce and some of this sauce on your prime rib, you are ready for a great Christmas Eve!

Gravy for Yorkshire Pudding

MAKES ABOUT 3 CUPS

3 cups Beef Stock (page 274)
4 tablespoons (½ stick) butter
½ cup all-purpose flour
1 tablespoon Maggi Liquid Seasoning
2 teaspoons Kitchen Bouquet
  Salt and freshly ground black pepper to taste

Bring the beef stock to a simmer in a 4-quart saucepan. In a small frying pan, melt the butter and add the flour. Cook together over low heat, stirring, until browned slightly, but do not burn. Stir the roux into the hot stock, using a wire whisk. Whisk and simmer until smooth. Add the Maggi, Kitchen Bouquet, and salt and pepper to taste.

I love my Yorkshire pudding with gravy on it. You can make your gravy from the pan drippings of the roast, of course, but sometimes you might want just to make a quick gravy for a quick dinner of quick Yorkshire pudding and cold beef. Who am I trying to kid? Make a big batch of this and keep it in the freezer.

CHRISTMAS
ROAST GOOSE DINNER

Roast Goose

Stuffing for Goose

Gravy for Goose

Red Cabbage

Baked Onions

Oven-Roasted Potatoes

This very English menu feels like Charles Dickens.
It remains a great favorite at our house.

Roast Goose

SERVES 6 TO 8

1 10-pound goose
   Salt and freshly ground black pepper to taste
1 tablespoon lemon juice
1 recipe Stuffing for Goose (page 206)

Remove the fat from the goose cavity and save for another use. Remove the neck and giblets and place in a small pot. Cut off the wing tips and add to the pot. Add enough cold water to cover, about 2½ cups. Bring to a boil and simmer, covered, 1½ hours. Discard the wing tips and the neck. Remove the giblets and grind or chop fine. Reserve the giblets for the stuffing and save the stock for the gravy.

Rub the inside of the goose with salt, pepper, and the lemon juice. Pack the cavity of the goose with the stuffing. Don't pack too tightly, any leftover stuffing can be baked separately. Close up the cavity, using poultry pins and string. Tie the legs together and tie the wings close to the body. Using a poultry pin, prick the skin of the goose all over. Place the goose, breast side down, on a rack inside a large roasting pan. Pour 2 cups of boiling water over the goose. Roast, uncovered, in a preheated 400° oven for 1 hour. Reduce the oven temperature to 350°. Remove the goose from the oven and discard the liquid in the bottom of the pan. Turn the goose over so that it is breast side up. Pour an additional 2 cups boiling water over the goose. Continue roasting the goose 1 hour longer at 350°. Remove the pan from the oven and pour off all the liquid again. Roast 1 hour longer or until nicely browned. Remove from the oven and let stand 15 to 20 minutes in a warm place before carving. Reserve the fat in the roasting pan to make Gravy for Goose (page 207).

People seem to be a bit nervous about roasting a goose, but it is really quite simple. Pouring boiling water over the bird a few times while it is roasting helps to get rid of much of the fat. It really works!

Stuffing for Goose

SERVES 6 TO 8

This dressing is very rich
in flavor due to the
richness of the goose. The
night after Christmas you
will find me sitting in
front of the refrigerator
eating dressing cold.

1 ½   pounds white bread, cubed and dried overnight
       Reserved cooked and ground giblets from Roast Goose (page 205)
2   tablespoons olive oil
4   tablespoons (½ stick) butter
3   cloves garlic, peeled and sliced
3   medium yellow onions, peeled and sliced
3   stalks celery, chopped
¼   cup chopped fresh parsley
1 ½   tablespoons dried sage, whole
2   cups Chicken Stock (page 275)
3   eggs, beaten
       Salt and freshly ground black pepper to taste

Heat a large frying pan and add the olive oil, butter, garlic, onions, celery, and parsley. Sauté until the vegetables are tender. In a large bowl, combine the dried bread cubes, sautéed vegetables, and all the remaining ingredients. Mix together until everything is evenly incorporated. Pack into the cavity of the goose.

Gravy for Goose

MAKES ABOUT 3 CUPS

3 tablespoons reserved fat from Roast
   Goose (page 205)

5 tablespoons all-purpose flour

4 cups reserved stock (giblet stock [page 205] plus
   enough Chicken Stock [page 275] to make 4 cups
   stock total)

¼ cup dry white wine

1 teaspoon Kitchen Bouquet

1 tablespoon Maggi Liquid Seasoning
   Salt and freshly ground black pepper to taste

Heat the reserved goose fat in a 2-quart saucepan and stir
in the flour. Cook over low heat for 2 minutes to form a
roux. Do not burn. Heat the stock and the wine in another
saucepan and add to the roux. Use a wire whisk for this
and whisk the whole time until a smooth sauce is achieved.
Simmer, uncovered, until reduced to about 3 cups. Add the
remaining ingredients and simmer the gravy a few minutes
more.

Red Cabbage

SERVES 6 TO 8

3 pounds red cabbage, cored and shredded
1 ½ cups Beef Stock (page 274)
½ cup firmly packed brown sugar
½ cup cider vinegar
4 tablespoons (½ stick) butter
¼ teaspoon freshly ground black pepper
Salt to taste

Combine all the ingredients, except the salt, in a 10- to 12-quart stainless-steel pot. Bring to a boil, stir, cover, and simmer over low heat, stirring occasionally, 1 hour and 15 minutes. Add salt to taste.

This is traditional with an English Christmas dinner since it was one of the major winter vegetables available in old London town. Your children will love the sweet flavor of this dish.

Baked Onions

SERVES 6 TO 8

6 medium yellow onions

2 quarts Chicken Stock (page 275)

3 tablespoons butter, melted

½ teaspoon paprika

¼ teaspoon freshly ground black pepper

¼ teaspoon salt

Crumb Topping

2 tablespoons butter, melted

⅓ cup bread crumbs

½ teaspoon salt

⅛ teaspoon dried thyme, whole

Peel the onions but leave them whole. Place the peeled onions in a large pot and add the chicken stock. Bring to a boil, cover, and simmer gently for 30 minutes. Carefully drain the onions, reserving the stock for another use. Place the onions in a shallow ovenproof baking dish so that they fit comfortably. Combine the melted butter, paprika, black pepper, and salt and pour the mixture over the onions. Turn the onions so that all are coated with the seasoned butter mixture. Bake in a preheated 400° oven for 15 minutes.

Mix together all the ingredients for the crumb topping and sprinkle it over the onions. Bake 15 minutes longer.

If you have never cooked such a dish for your family, get ready for a surprise. They are all going to love it!

Oven-Roasted Potatoes

SERVES 8

You will appreciate this dish more often than at Christmas. You don't have to watch these very carefully and they keep well in the warming oven.

4   pounds baking potatoes
½   cup (1 stick) butter, melted
½   teaspoon salt
¼   teaspoon freshly ground black pepper
¼   teaspoon sweet paprika
2   cloves garlic, peeled and crushed
½   cup Chicken Stock (page 275)
    Flour for dusting, if desired

Peel the potatoes and quarter them lengthwise. Place the potatoes in a 13 x 9-inch baking dish or sheet pan. Add the remaining ingredients, except the chicken stock. Turn the potatoes to coat them evenly. Bake in a preheated 350° oven for 1 hour. Add the chicken stock and bake 1 hour longer, turning the potatoes a few times during cooking. You may also dust the potatoes with a little flour toward the end of the cooking time and place under the broiler for a nice browned effect.

CHRISTMAS
CROWN ROAST OF PORK
DINNER

Crown Roast of Pork

Stuffing for Crown Roast of Pork

Gravy

Cold Asparagus

Brussels Sprouts with Balsamic Vinegar

Crown Roast of Pork

SERVES 8

1   crown roast of pork
    Freshly ground black pepper to taste
1   tablespoon dried sage, whole
1   tablespoon dried thyme, whole
1½ cups dry white wine for basting
    Salt to taste
    Dressing for the Pork (optional) (page 218)

For this dish you must find a real, live butcher. Have him cut and tie a crown roast of pork for you. He will understand what to do. You will have a roast of 16 ribs, enough for 8 persons.

Rub the roast with freshly ground pepper, and the sage and thyme. Wrap the ends of the ribs in aluminum foil so that they will not burn during roasting. Place a ball of loosely crumpled aluminum foil in the center of the roast. Place the roast on a rack in a roasting pan. Bake in a preheated 325° oven for about 25 minutes per pound. I use a meat thermometer and roast the meat until it reaches an internal temperature of 165°. Baste from time to time with the wine. Allow the roast to sit a few minutes before you carve it. When ready to serve, remove the foil and place a large bouquet of parsley in the center of the roast. You may also fill the center with dressing. Salt to taste. You may wish to put little paper panties (see illustrations page 219) on the rib ends. If you want to serve the crown with gravy, use the pan drippings to make your favorite or follow the directions for Gravy for Goose (page 207). I love the taste of pork so much, I like just to pick it up, dressed with its panty, and enjoy it naturally.

Crown Roast of Pork is a delight to eat because it is so very moist, but it is also great fun to serve as it is so festive and attractive. Prepare little paper panties (page 219) or purchase them in a gourmet shop. These will add some color to the table.

You might want to fill the center of the crown with this bread dressing. Bake the dressing in a covered casserole and then fill the cavity of the cooked roast just before serving. Do not bake the dressing in the roast.

Stuffing for Crown Roast of Pork

2	tablespoons olive oil
4	tablespoons (½ stick) butter
3	cloves garlic, peeled and sliced
3	medium yellow onions, peeled and sliced
3	stalks celery, chopped
¼	cup chopped fresh parsley
1	pound cooked breakfast or Italian sausage, coarsely chopped
1½	tablespoons dried sage, whole
2	cups Chicken Stock (page 275)
3	eggs, beaten
	Salt and freshly ground black pepper to taste

Heat a large frying pan and add the olive oil, butter, garlic, onions, celery, and parsley. Sauté until the vegetables are tender. In a large bowl, combine the dried bread cubes, sautéed vegetables, and all the remaining ingredients. Mix together until everything is evenly incorporated. Bake in a covered casserole at 350° for 1 hour. Fill the center of the cooked crown roast with the cooked dressing.

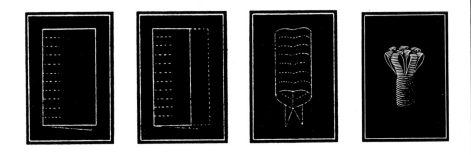

How to Make Panties for Meat and Poultry

1. Make little cuts along the seam of a paper napkin (each about ⅛ inch apart and about 1¼ inches deep).

2. Cut away all the napkin except a 1-inch border under the cuts.

3. Reverse the fold of the cuts and roll the panties around your thumb. Seal with Scotch tape. You will need to experiment a bit to learn to make them the proper diameter for whatever kind of meat or poultry you wish to decorate.

Cold Asparagus

SERVES 6 TO 8

1 ½   pounds fresh asparagus

2   tablespoons olive oil

The Dressing

½   cup extra virgin olive oil

1   tablespoon white wine vinegar

1   tablespoon fresh lemon juice

Salt and freshly ground black pepper to taste

Break off the tough woody ends of the asparagus spears. Bring a large pot of water to a boil. Add the 2 tablespoons of olive oil and the asparagus. Blanch the asparagus only 2 minutes if they are of medium thickness. Do not overcook! Drain in a colander and immediately rinse under ice-cold water. Drain well and place on a platter.

In a bowl, mix all the ingredients for the dressing together well and pour over the asparagus. Cover with plastic wrap. Chill the asparagus, turning them once, for 2 hours.

This is great with the Crown Roast of Pork. Yes, I know that fresh asparagus is very expensive in December, but what a delight for the festival table. In the winter you may wind up using frozen asparagus for this dish. Do not overcook it.

Brussels Sprouts with Balsamic Vinegar

SERVES 6 TO 8

1 ½   **pounds fresh Brussels sprouts**

   2   **tablespoons olive oil**

   2   **cloves garlic, peeled and sliced**

   1   **medium yellow onion, peeled and thinly sliced**

  ¼   **cup balsamic vinegar**

   2   **tablespoons butter**

        Salt and freshly ground black pepper to taste

Trim off the stems and remove any limp leaves from the Brussels sprouts. Blanch the sprouts in boiling water to cover for 5 minutes. Drain and rinse under cold water to stop the cooking.

Heat a large frying pan and add the olive oil, garlic, and onion. Sauté a few minutes until the onion just becomes tender. Add the blanched drained Brussels sprouts. Sauté a few minutes until the Brussels sprouts are cooked to your liking. Add the vinegar and toss so that all the sprouts are coated with the vinegar. Add the butter and salt and pepper to taste and toss together again.

This delicious variation on the winter sprout will change some minds in your house. Those who are convinced that they do not like Brussels sprouts will enjoy these. Be sure not to overcook them.

The following menu is
unusually good. It has a
great deal of color and
enough new dishes to
interest everyone.
It is Craig
Wollam's favorite.
He is Jeff's
chef.

CHRISTMAS
RACK OF LAMB
DINNER

Rack of Lamb

**Sautéed Red and Green
Bell Peppers**

Bulgur Pesto Timbales

**Mushroom Shallot Sauce
for Lamb**

Nellie's Lemon Tart

Rack of Lamb

S E R V E S 6

2   racks of lamb (approximately 1 ½ pounds per rack)
    Salt and freshly ground black pepper to taste
3   tablespoons Dijon-style mustard
½   cup (1 stick) butter
2   cloves garlic, peeled and minced
1   cup plain bread crumbs
2   tablespoons finely chopped fresh parsley

Season the racks of lamb with salt and pepper. Heat a heavy frying pan and brown the fat on the top of the lamb over high heat. This will take 1 or 2 minutes and no oil is needed. Remove the meat from the pan and allow to cool. Rub the meat (not the bones) of each rack with 1 ½ tablespoons of the mustard. Set aside.

In another frying pan, heat the butter and in it sauté the garlic a few seconds. Remove from the heat and stir in the bread crumbs and parsley. Coat the meat with the bread crumb mixture by rolling the racks of lamb directly in the frying pan of bread crumbs. There should be a coating of bread crumbs on the meat only, not on the bones. Place the racks on a rack in a shallow roasting pan. Roast in a preheated 450° oven for 15 minutes for rare. (Add 10 minutes if you like it medium but be careful not to overcook.) Remove the pan from the oven and allow the meat to stand in a warm place (but not on top of the stove!) for 5 minutes. Slice into individual bone sections and serve at once. Serve with Mushroom Shallot Wine Sauce (page 234).

This is my cook's favorite Christmas dish. Craig's mother, Karen, is a fine cook in her own right, and she has been feeding her family Christmas Rack of Lamb for years.

Sautéed Red and Green Bell Peppers

SERVES 6 TO 8

This not only looks like Christmas but it tastes like Christmas! Do not overcook the peppers.

4 medium red bell peppers

4 medium green bell peppers

3 tablespoons olive oil

3 cloves garlic, peeled and sliced

1 medium yellow onion, peeled and sliced

1 teaspoon dried oregano, whole

1 teaspoon dried rosemary, whole

$1/3$ cup dry red wine

Salt and freshly ground black pepper to taste

$1/4$ cup chopped fresh parsley

Core both the red and green peppers and cut into large strips; set aside. Heat a large frying pan and add the olive oil, garlic, and onion. Sauté a few minutes until the onion begins to collapse. Add the bell peppers, oregano, and rosemary, and sauté 5 minutes. Add the wine and continue cooking until the peppers are tender. Add salt and pepper to taste and the parsley and toss together.

Bulgur Pesto Timbales

MAKES 6 TO 8, DEPENDING ON
THE SIZE OF THE MOLDS

1 cup coarse-grain bulgur wheat

2 cups Chicken Stock (page 275)

½ cup orzo pasta (find in Italian or Greek markets)

3 green onions, chopped

¼ cup pine nuts, toasted

1 tablespoon chopped fresh parsley

2 eggs, beaten

¼ cup whipping cream

2 tablespoons pesto (buy in a glass jar or frozen at the market)

Salt and freshly ground black pepper to taste

I thought this dish up one day for a formal dinner party and now everybody is loving it. I think you will too.

Combine the bulgur and the chicken stock in a small sauce-pan. Bring to a boil and simmer, covered, 15 minutes until the bulgur has absorbed the stock. Set aside.

In another small saucepan, bring 2 cups of water to a boil. Add the orzo and cook until just tender. Drain well and set aside to cool.

Combine the cooked bulgur, drained orzo, and the remaining ingredients in a mixing bowl. Pack the mixture into well-greased timbale molds and place in a baking pan. Fill the pan with hot water so that it comes one third of the way up the sides of the molds. Bake, uncovered, in a 375° oven for 45 minutes. Remove the baking pan from the oven and remove the molds from the pan. Invert the timbales onto plates. If you have any trouble getting the timbales out, run the blade of a table knife around the inside of the molds.

Mushroom Shallot Sauce for Lamb

MAKES ABOUT 4 CUPS

½ ounce dried porcini mushrooms (or dried South American-type)

3 cups Beef Stock (page 274)

2 cups Chicken Stock (page 275)

½ cup dry red wine

1 tablespoon butter

1 tablespoon olive oil

½ cup minced shallots

½ pound fresh mushrooms, chopped

2 tablespoons chopped fresh mint

Salt and freshly ground black pepper to taste

In a small bowl, soak the dried mushrooms in ¾ cup warm water for 45 minutes. Drain and chop the mushrooms, discarding the liquid. In a small pot, combine the beef stock, chicken stock, and wine and simmer, uncovered, for 20 minutes. Heat a frying pan and add the butter, olive oil, and shallots. Sauté until the shallots are tender. Add the fresh mushrooms to the pan and sauté until tender. Add the drained and chopped dried mushrooms to the pot of stock, along with the sautéed mushroom mixture. Simmer gently, uncovered, for 1 hour. Add the mint and salt and pepper to taste.

Nellie's Lemon Tart

SERVES 8

The Dough

3/4 cup (1 1/2 sticks) butter, at room temperature

3 tablespoons confectioners' sugar

1 1/2 cups all-purpose flour

The Filling

2 eggs, at room temperature

3/4 cup granulated sugar

Grated peel of 2 lemons

Juice of 2 lemons (use the lemons you just grated)

3/4 cup (1 1/2 sticks) butter, at room temperature

Garnish

1 lemon

Granulated sugar for sprinkling

This tart is a classic finish for a very rich meal. It is the gift of Dr. Nellie Campbell, a dear friend of mine from Toulouse, France. It will become a favorite, I know.

Cream together the butter and confectioners' sugar for the dough (I use my KitchenAid mixer). Add the flour and blend until coarse and grainy. Place the dough in a plastic bag and refrigerate 30 minutes. Press the dough onto the bottom and sides of a 10-inch tart pan. Bake the pastry shell in a preheated 425° oven for 10 minutes. Remove and cool.

Blend together the eggs and the granulated sugar. Add the grated peel, lemon juice, and butter and mix well. Place the tart pan on a cookie sheet and pour the filling into the pastry shell. Peel the outer rind off another lemon so that only a thin layer of white pith remains (a potato peeler works well for this). Cut 8 thin slices from the peeled lemon and carefully place the slices in eighths on the tart.

Bake in a 350° oven for 35 minutes. Remove from the oven and sprinkle a little granulated sugar on the slices of

lemon on the tart. Turn the oven to high broil. Place the tart under the broiler on the top rack and allow to brown slightly on top. Watch this closely so that you don't burn the crust. Allow to cool completely. You can also use a blowtorch to add an attractive browning to the top of the tart.

CHRISTMAS
IN OTHER
CULTURES

A SWEDISH
WINTER FEAST

Swedish Corned Pork Roast

Swedish Sauerkraut

**Swedish Green Split Peas
with Bacon**

**Mashed Rutabaga,
Turnip, and Potato**

Sweet and Hot Mustard

Rye Bread

This is a hearty meal for the darkest night of the year.
During the winter the Swedes eat pickled meats and many
root vegetables. This whole meal is very typical of the food
that requires a glass of aquavit in order to get it all down.
This has become one of my favorite Christmas menus.

Swedish Corned Pork Roast

SERVES 12 TO 16

To Corn the Roast

- 2 gallons water
- 1 pound pickling salt
- 1 teaspoon saltpeter
- 8 pounds boneless pork butt, tied

- 2 bay leaves
- 15 whole peppercorns
- 5 whole allspice

In a large stainless steel-pot or pickling crock, mix the water, pickling salt, and saltpeter together until dissolved. Untie the pork roast and place in the pickling solution. Place a heavy plate on top of the pork so that it will remain submerged. Cover, and refrigerate for 10 days. Check occasionally to be sure the pork is covered by the liquid.

After 10 days, remove the pork and retie it into a roast. Rinse well with fresh water. Place the roast in a large kettle, cover with cold water, and add the remaining ingredients. Bring to a boil, cover, and simmer 2 hours and 15 minutes. Slice the pork and place on a large platter. Serve with Sweet and Hot Mustard (page 250).

Please note that this dish takes ten days of pickling time, but it is well worth the effort. If you prefer to buy a corned or pickled fresh ham, a Swedish market will have such a thing for you if you order well before Christmas. The Paulina Market in Chicago makes a terrific corned fresh ham.

Swedish Sauerkraut

SERVES 6 TO 8

1 pound smoked pork jowl, diced

2 medium yellow onions, peeled and sliced

1 pound green cabbage, cored and shredded

2 quarts sauerkraut (packed in a glass jar)

1 apple, cored and coarsely chopped

2 cups dry white wine

1 tablespoon light brown sugar

1 teaspoon caraway seeds

1 teaspoon freshly ground black pepper, or to taste

Heat a 4- to 6-quart pot and add the diced pork jowl. Brown the jowl to render most of its fat. Remove the pieces of pork from the pot and set aside. Pour off most of the fat, leaving 2 tablespoons in the pot. Add the onions to the pot and sauté a few minutes. Add the cabbage and reserved cooked jowl and cook, covered, 5 minutes until the cabbage collapses. Rinse the sauerkraut in a colander and squeeze dry. Add the sauerkraut to the pot with the remaining ingredients and combine. Cover and simmer gently for 1 hour, stirring occasionally.

The peoples of northern Europe and Scandinavia all seem to love sauerkraut. It is best if you can buy it fresh from the barrel, but that is getting hard to find. Sometimes you can find a fresh product packed in a plastic pouch, or stick to glass. I swear I can taste the can if you offer me 'kraut from a tin.

Swedish Green Split Peas with Bacon

SERVES 8

½ pound bacon, chopped

1 medium yellow onion, peeled and sliced

1 pound green split peas, washed and soaked in 6 cups water for 6 hours or overnight

Salt and freshly ground black pepper to taste

4 tablespoons (½ stick) butter

Brown the bacon in a frying pan. Remove the bacon and set aside. Discard all but 2 tablespoons of the fat in a pan. Heat the reserved fat in the frying pan and add the onion. Sauté until tender.

Drain the peas and place in a 4- to 6-quart pot along with the reserved bacon and sautéed onions. Add enough fresh water to just cover the peas. Bring to a boil and simmer, covered, about 1½ hours, or until the water is absorbed and the peas are thick. Stir occasionally to prevent sticking and add more water if necessary. Stir in salt and pepper to taste and the butter.

Such a good dish, and certainly basic. You can also do this with yellow split peas, another dish the Swedes would enjoy.

Mashed Rutabaga, Turnip, and Potato

SERVES 8

1 ¾   pounds rutabaga, peeled and quartered
1 ½   pounds turnips, peeled and quartered
   1   pound russet potatoes, peeled and quartered
   ¼   cup (½ stick) butter, melted
   ½   cup whipping cream
        Salt and freshly ground pepper to taste

The vegetables can be peeled ahead of time if you hold them in separate containers covered with water and Fruit-Fresh to prevent browning. Drain before cooking. Place the drained rutabaga in a 6-quart pot with ample fresh water and a pinch of salt. Boil 15 minutes. Add the turnips, and potatoes and boil 15 minutes more, until all the vegetables are tender. Drain well. Mash the vegetables with the remaining ingredients. You can also purée them in several batches in a good food processor.

I *told you that the Swedes enjoy root vegetables in the winter. Here three are blended, and the result is very mild and delicious.*

Sweet and Hot Mustard

MAKES ABOUT 2 CUPS

This wonderful mustard is a gift from Pearlie and Lester Baskin. It will keep, refrigerated, for a week and you will come to love the stuff on all sorts of meats. It is just perfect with this corned pork roast.

1 4-ounce can dry Colman's mustard
1 cup malt vinegar
1 cup sugar
6 eggs, beaten

In a small stainless-steel bowl, mix the mustard and the vinegar until smooth. Allow to sit on the counter for 3 hours. Combine the mustard mixture with the sugar and eggs in the top of a double boiler. Add cold water to the bottom pan of the double boiler. Bring to a gentle simmer and cook 20 to 25 minutes, stirring regularly until thickened (the consistency of mayonnaise). Store in the refrigerator.

French Oysters
for Christmas Eve

There are so many possible dishes for a French Christmas Eve that I really could not decide what would be most typical. My French friend Dr. Nellie Campbell told me that oysters on the half shell would be on almost every holiday table.

The French delight in a shallot sauce along with some fine wine . . . and the oysters. This would be the first course for a great Christmas Eve celebration.

You might want to add the oysters to the Christmas Rack of Lamb menu (pages 192–201) for a very nice French evening.

Shallot Sauce for Oysters

MAKES ABOUT $1/2$ CUP

1	teaspoon freshly ground coarse black pepper
	Juice of 2 lemons
1	tablespoon red wine vinegar
1 $1/2$	tablespoons minced shallots

In a small bowl, combine all the ingredients and chill. Serve with raw oysters on the half shell.

This was quickly developed by Craig, my right-hand man. He uses a bit more black pepper in his sauce so the flavor is bright.

ITALIAN
CHRISTMAS EVE

Pasta with Seafood

Salad

Panettone

Italian
Christmas Eve

Christmas Eve is considered a fasting day in most of Italy, so meat is not served. However, leave it to the Italians to develop a seafood dish that is so delicious that you forget about meat.

The dish is made with seven different seafoods, and I assume the number refers to the seven sacraments. It took me a bit of research to come up with all seven of them because I am always forgetting one. Here is the list: Baptism, Confirmation, Eucharist, Absolution, Holy Orders, Marriage, and Extreme Unction. Now you know.

Add a green salad to this meal, and perhaps some Sautéed Red and Green Peppers (page 230), and you will have a grand time. A traditional dessert would be panettone, a light fruit bread, much lighter than fruitcake. A cup of black coffee and you are ready for Saint Nicholaus.

Pasta with Seafood

SERVES 8 TO 10 AS A MAIN COURSE

½	pound baccalà (dried salt cod), cut in 1-inch pieces, rinsed, and soaked (see below)
3	cloves garlic, peeled and sliced
½	cup olive oil
1	cup dry white wine
4 to 6	cups Italian Tomato Sauce (page 261)
¾	pound littleneck or cherrystone clams, rinsed and drained (be sure the clams are closed tight and none are filled with mud)
¾	pound mussels, beards removed, rinsed, and drained
½	pound crab claws
½	pound fresh cod
½	pound medium shrimp, peeled
½	pounds squid, cleaned and cut into ½-inch rings
2	pounds penne or linguine pasta

For the baccalà: Rinse the baccalà several times and soak it in plenty of cold water for a minimum of 12 hours. Change the water a few times during the soaking process. Drain well. The cod is ready to use.

Bring a large pot of water to a boil to cook the pasta. In another large pot, sauté the garlic in the olive oil for 1 minute. Add the wine and tomato sauce. Simmer gently, covered, for 5 minutes. Stir in the baccalà, clams, mussels, crab claws, and the fresh cod. Cover and simmer until the clams and mussels just begin to open. Add the shrimp and squid and simmer about 2 minutes until the shrimp turn pink and are barely cooked through. At the same time, cook the pasta in the boiling water with a pinch of salt until *al dente*. When the pasta is cooked and the seafood is done, drain the pasta well and place on a large platter. Discard any shellfish with unopened shells. Pour the cooked seafood and the sauce over the pasta.

Italian Tomato Sauce

MAKES 3 QUARTS

2   28-ounce cans tomato purée

1   6-ounce can tomato paste

1   quart Chicken Stock (page 275)

2   cups dry red wine

¼   cup olive oil

2   yellow onions, peeled and minced

6   cloves garlic, peeled and chopped fine

2   ribs celery, with leaves, minced

1   unpeeled carrot, grated

½   cup chopped fresh parsley

½   pound fresh mushrooms, chopped

½   teaspoon crushed red pepper flakes

1   tablespoon dried oregano, whole

1   teaspoon dried rosemary, whole

1   tablespoon dried basil, whole, or 2 tablespoons chopped fresh

2   whole cloves

½   teaspoon freshly ground black pepper, or to taste

2   tablespoons salt, or to taste

1   teaspoon sugar

Place the tomato purée, tomato paste, chicken stock, and wine in a large pot. Heat a frying pan and add the olive oil. In it sauté the onions, garlic, celery, and carrot until they just begin to brown a bit. Add the vegetables to the tomato mixture with all the remaining ingredients. Bring to a gentle boil, then reduce to a simmer. Simmer for 2 hours, partly covered, stirring occasionally. Store in the refrigerator in plastic, glass, or stainless-steel containers—never aluminum. The sauce will keep for a week in the refrigerator.

Keep some of this on hand in your freezer as it is very versatile. Best when fresh, however.

Panettone

MAKES 1 OR 2 TALL LOAVES

3 packages dry yeast

½ cup warm water (105°–115°)

Pinch of sugar

6 egg yolks, at room temperature

1 teaspoon vanilla

½ teaspoon salt

⅓ cup sugar

2 to 3 cups all-purpose flour

½ cup (1 stick) butter, at room temperature, cut into 10 pieces

⅓ cup diced Candied Orange or Lemon Peel (page 270) (optional)

¼ cup raisins

2 tablespoons melted butter to brush loaf

In a small bowl, combine the yeast, water, and sugar. Set aside in a draft-free spot until the mixture is full of bubbles. Pour the mixture into a large bowl. Stir in the egg yolks, vanilla, salt, and sugar. Blend in 2 cups of flour, ½ cup at a time, and beat until the dough pulls away from the sides in strands. Cut the butter into the dough.

Add the candied peel and raisins. Add about 1 cup more of the flour, a little at a time, mixing it now with your hands. The dough should be firm, not sticky.

Turn the dough onto a lightly floured board, and knead until it is smooth and shiny.

Put the dough back in the bowl and smear a little butter all over to keep the surface from crusting. Cover the bowl with plastic wrap and let sit in a warm place (80°–85°) until the dough rises to about double its original size.

Good packaged panettone, made in Italy, are found in the market at Christmas. Making it at home takes a lot of time, but some of you may want to make it. Use the candied peel recipe on page 270.

263

Grease 1 large or 2 small coffee cans, or a panettone pan. The cans will be about half filled with dough. Cover lightly with wax paper and return to the warm place until the dough has doubled in bulk—near but not over the top of the rim of the can. Preheat the oven to 400°. Remove the middle shelf.

Brush the top of the dough with melted butter. Bake the loaf or loaves on the bottom shelf in a hot oven for 10 minutes. Reduce the heat to 350° and bake for an additional 30 to 40 minutes. Halfway through the baking, brush again with the butter and rotate the tins. The loaves will be crisp and brown when they are done. Pierce with a metal skewer; if it comes clean, the loaf is done. If the loaf tests done but the sides are not brown enough, unmold and return to the oven for another 5 or 10 minutes. Watch closely so it doesn't overbrown.

Remove the bread from the oven. Handle the tall loaf or loaves with special care while they are hot; they are somewhat delicate. Place on a wire rack until they are cool. Panettone stays fresh for a long time, if it is well wrapped.

CHRISTMAS EVE
TREE TRIMMING

Christmas Eve Pasta
Penne with Peas and Red Bell Pepper

SERVES 4 TO 6

3   tablespoons olive oil

2   cloves garlic, peeled and crushed

1   cup peeled and sliced yellow onions

1   cup julienned red bell pepper

¼   cup chopped fresh parsley

3   eggs, beaten

2   cups half-and-half

1   10-ounce package frozen peas, thawed

1   pound penne

½   cup chopped fresh basil

¼   cup grated Parmesan cheese

    Salt and freshly ground black pepper to taste

Heat a large frying pan and add the olive oil, garlic, onions, bell pepper, and parsley. Sauté until tender. Bring a large pot of water with a pinch of salt to a boil. In a small bowl, beat the eggs together with the half-and-half and set aside. Place a colander in the sink and put the thawed peas in it. Cook the pasta in the boiling salted water until *al dente* and drain it into the colander onto the peas (this will cook the peas sufficiently). Return the drained pasta and peas to the pot and add the sautéed vegetables, basil, egg and half-and-half mixture, and Parmesan cheese. Toss this all together and serve immediately.

It is the colors that give this dish a Christmas Eve feeling. Simply add this dish to your traditional menu, and it will become a part of your family's traditions.

269

Candied Orange or Lemon Peel

MAKES ABOUT 2 QUARTS ORANGE
OR ABOUT 1 1/2 QUARTS LEMON PEEL

This is a Christmas treat that goes back to the early days in this culture when even the peel of a holiday orange was not wasted. If your children have never tasted freshly candied peel, they are in for a serious treat.

8   navel oranges (about 4 1/2 pounds) or 14 lemons (about 4 1/2 pounds)
4   cups granulated sugar
1   cup water

Using a paring knife, quarter the fruit lengthwise, cutting through the peel only. Remove each quarter of peel from the fruit. Save the flesh of the fruit for another use. Place the peels in a 4- to 6-quart pot and cover with cold water. Bring to a boil, uncovered, and simmer for 10 minutes. Drain and allow to cool. Using a tablespoon, carefully dig out most of the white pith on the peels and discard. Julienne the peels lengthwise into 1/4-inch strips and set aside.

Return the pot to the burner and add 2 cups of the sugar and the 1 cup water. Heat to dissolve the sugar. Add the julienned peel and simmer gently, covered, 45 minutes. Stir occasionally. Remove the peel to drain on a fine mesh cooling rack with a pan underneath. Spread the peel out so it will drain evenly. Allow to cool and dry out 1 hour. Place the drained dried peel in a large bowl and toss with the remaining 2 cups sugar until evenly coated. Sift the excess sugar through your hands. Place the sugar-coated peel on a baking sheet and allow to dry overnight. Store in canning jars up to 2 weeks.

Hot Buttered Rum Mix

SERVES THE NEIGHBORHOOD

1 pound light brown sugar

1 pound confectioners' sugar

1/2 pound (2 sticks) butter, at room temperature

1 quart vanilla ice cream, slightly melted

Light rum

Ground nutmeg for garnish

In a large bowl, blend the first four ingredients together well (I use my KitchenAid mixer). Add rum to taste and garnish with nutmeg.

To make 1 drink, put 2 tablespoons of the ice cream mixture in a mug. Add 1 jigger of rum and fill the mug with boiling water. Garnish the top with the nutmeg. Freeze the remaining ice cream mixture in a plastic container for future use.

This is a great favorite at our holiday house. Patty, my wife, began making this when the boys were very tiny. I would put up the Christmas tree, and Patty would make the two of us a Hot Buttered Rum. The boys would get out their little Santa Claus cups and have Hot Buttereds, no rum, of course. This drink is very good without the rum, so everyone in the house can get in on the act.

Beef Stock

MAKES 5 QUARTS

It is impossible for me to operate a kitchen without this basic necessity. This is far superior to any canned or instant stock that you might buy.

5   pounds bare beef rendering bones, sawed into 2-inch pieces
1   bunch of carrots, unpeeled and chopped
1   bunch of celery, chopped
3   yellow onions, unpeeled and chopped

Tell your butcher that you need bare rendering bones. They should not have any meat on them at all, so they should be cheap. Have him saw them into 2-inch pieces.

Roast the bones in an uncovered pan at 400° for 2 hours. Be careful with this because your own oven may be a bit too hot. Watch the bones, which you want to be toasty brown, not black.

Place the roasted bones, along with the fat, in a soup pot and add 1 quart of water for each pound of bones. For 5 pounds of bones, add 1 bunch of carrots, chopped; 1 bunch of celery, chopped; 3 yellow onions, chopped with peel and all. (The peel will give a lovely color to the stock.)

Bring to a simmer, uncovered, and cook for 12 hours. You may need to add water to keep the soup up to the same level. Do not salt the stock.

Strain the stock, and store in the refrigerator. Allow the fat to stay on the top of the stock when you refrigerate it; the fat will seal the stock and allow you to keep it for several days.

Chicken Stock

MAKES ABOUT 3 QUARTS

3   pounds chicken backs and necks

3   quarts cold water

4   ribs celery, coarsely chopped

6   carrots, unpeeled, sliced thick

2   medium yellow onions, peeled and quartered

8   whole black peppercorns

Place the chicken backs and necks in a soup pot and rinse with very hot tap water. Drain and add the cold water to the pot, along with the other ingredients. Bring to a simmer and cook for 2 hours. Be sure to skim off the froth that forms when the pot first comes to a simmer.

The stock will taste a bit flat to you since it has no salt. Salt will be added when you use the stock in the preparation of soups, sauces, or stews.

Another kitchen necessity, Chicken Stock is easy to make and not filled with salt like commercial stock and cubes.

Epilogue
The Problem with Christmas

Now it is time to be terribly honest with one another. While Christmas is surely the most beautiful holiday for us, it is also a time of incredible tension and letdown. Why does this happen?

Once Christmas is over, there is a certain feeling that we have worked too hard for a two-day holiday: This year was to be different, and we were going to be kind to everyone. We are exhausted and we have failed to get along with all of our relatives. The place is a mess, and we are up to

our necks in debt, and the kids have already broken a very expensive toy.

All of us have these feelings. It is not just you.

What is the problem with Christmas? I think it stems from the fact that we always feel that the success of Christmas depends upon us, and we never seem to meet our own expectations. That is our style!

"What a meal I have cooked, and now they are going to be late."

"Oh, drat. The snow is going to ruin everything."

"I told you that this Christmas tree was crooked!"

"I know, honey, I will just have to calm down until your brother-in-law-leaves."

"While shepherds watched their flocks by night. . . ."

We want peace and quiet and perfection in entertaining. The Bible wants peace, and that means fulfillment for all persons, not just lack of war. In the midst of the darkest night of the year we have attempted to turn the Christmas

into our holiday of light, dependent upon our own successes, but that is not the meaning of the Christmas. We suffer from Post-Christmas Depression because on our own Christmas does not work. It is not the tree, or the dinner, or the planning, or the weather, or the relatives that make the Mass of the Christ. It is the Child. Come to the manger and be amazed. God is confessing His/Her love for us. How utterly amazing. God comes to us as the Baby in swaddling clothes.

I pray you, do not return to the comfort of the Lighted Tree as if it were the answer in the dark winter. The tree must be taken down.

Come instead and see the Child. Here is the Peace that we are seeking, and here is the answer to the Christmas Problem.

"Glory to God in the Highest, and on earth
peace among men and women with whom He
is pleased."

Merry Christmas, and I bid you and yours Peace.
Jeff Smith

Christmas Oratorio

W. H. Auden

Well, so that is that. Now we must dismantle the tree,

Putting the decorations back into their cardboard boxes—

Some have gotten broken—and carrying them up
    to the attic.

The holly and the mistletoe must be taken down and
    burnt,

And the children got ready for school. There are enough

Left-overs to do, warmed-up, for the rest of the week—

Not that we have much appetite, having drunk such
    a lot,

Stayed up so late, attempted—quite unsuccessfully—

To love all our relatives, and in general

Grossly overestimated our powers. Once again

As in previous years we have seen the actual Vision and
    failed.

To do more than entertain it as an agreeable

Possibility—once again we have sent Him away,

Begging though to remain His disobedient servant,

The promising child who cannot keep His word for long.

The Christmas Feast is already a fading memory,

And already the mind begins to be vaguely aware

Of an unpleasant whiff of apprehension at the thought

Of Lent and Good Friday which cannot, after all, now

Be very far off. But, for the time being, here we all are,

Back in the moderate Aristotelian city

Of darning and the Eight-Fifteen, where Euclid's
    geometry

And Newton's mechanics would account for our
    experience,

And the kitchen table exists because I scrub it.

It seems to have shrunk during the holidays. The streets

Are much narrower than we remembered; we had
    forgotten

The office was as depressing as this. To those who have
    seen

The Child, however dimly, however incredulously,

The Time Being is, in a sense, the most trying time
    of all.

For the innocent children who whispered so excitedly

Outside the locked door where they knew the presents
        to be

Grew up when it opened. Now, recollecting that moment

We can repress the joy, but the guilt remains conscious;

Remembering the stable where for once in our lives

Everything became a You and nothing was an It.

And craving the sensation but ignoring the cause,

We look round for something, no matter what, to inhibit

Our self-reflection, and the obvious thing for that purpose

Would be some great suffering. So, once we have met
        the Son,

We are tempted ever to pray to the Father;

"Lead us into temptation and evil for our sake."

They will come, all right, don't worry; probably
        in a form

That we do no expect, and certainly with a force

More dreadful than we can imagine. In the meantime

There are bills to be paid, machines to keep in repair,

Irregular verbs to learn, the Time Being to redeem

From insignificance. The happy morning is over,

The night of agony still to come; the time is noon:

When the Spirit must practise his scales of rejoicing

Without even a hostile audience, and the Soul endure

A silence that is neither for nor against her faith

That God's Will will be done, that, in spite of her
*   prayers,*

God will cheat no one, not even the world of its triumph.

Bibliography

Auld, William Muir. *Christmas Traditions*. New York: Macmillan, 1937.

Barnett, James H. *The American Christmas*. New York: Macmillan, 1954.

Black, Naomi, ed. *The Whole Christmas Catalog*. New York: HP Books, 1987.

Book of Christmas. New York: Time Life/Prentice Hall, 1987.

Coffin, Tristan P., ed. *The Book of Christmas Folklore*. New York: Seabury Press, 1973.

Cole, Joanna. *A Gift from Saint Francis*. New York: Morrow Junior Books, 1989.

Del Re, Gerard, and Patricia. *The Christmas Almanack.* New York: Doubleday, 1979.

Ebon, Martin. *Saint Nicholas: Life and Legend.* New York: Harper & Row, 1975.

Engle, Fannie, and Gertrude Blair. *The Jewish Festival Cookbook.* New York: David McKay, 1954.

Gardner, Horace J. *Let's Celebrate Christmas.* New York: A. S. Barnes, 1940.

Goodman, Naomi, et al. *The Good Book Cookbook: A Taste of the Biblical Past.* New York: Dodd, Mead, 1986.

Hadfield, Miles and John. *The Twelve Days of Christmas.* Boston: Little, Brown, 1962.

Jones, Barry, and M. V. Dixon. *Dictionary of Biography.* New York: St. Martin's, 1986.

Kainen, Ruth Cole. *America's Christmas Heritage: Christmas Folklore, Holiday Customs, and Recipes from All over the World.* New York: Funk & Wagnall's, 1969.

McNight, George H. *St. Nicholas.* New York: G. P. Putnam's, 1917.

McSpadden, J. Walker. *The Book of Holidays.* New York: Thomas Crowell, 1940.

Reader's Digest Book of Christmas. Pleasantville, N.Y.: Reader's Digest Association, 1973.

Rombauer, Irma S., and Marion R. Becker. *The Joy of Cooking.* Indianapolis: Bobbs-Merrill, 1972.

Sansom, William. *A Book of Christmas.* New York: McGraw-Hill, 1968.

Singer, Isaac Bashevis. *When Shlemiel Went to Warsaw & Other Stories.* New York: Farrar, Straus, Giroux, 1968.

Watts, Franklin, ed. *The Complete Christmas Books.* New York: Franklin Watts, 1958.

Index

Numbers in **boldface** type refer to recipes.

A NOTE ABOUT THE AUTHOR

Jeff Smith is an ordained Methodist minister who has brought his ministry to millions of TV viewers. His cooking shows rival network prime-time programs, reaching fifteen million households weekly. He lives in Tacoma, Washington.